THE SUCCESSFUL CLASSROOM

Management Strategies for Regular and Special Education Teachers

THE SUCCESSFUL CLASSROOM

Management Strategies for Regular and Special Education Teachers

DORIS PRONIN FROMBERG
MARYANNE DRISCOLL

Teachers College, Columbia University
New York and London

Published by Teachers College Press, 1234 Amsterdam Avenue,
New York, N.Y. 10027

Library of Congress Cataloging in Publication Data

Fromberg, Doris Pronin, 1937–
  The successful classroom.

  Bibliography: p.
  Includes index.
  1. Classroom management. 2. Elementary school teaching. 3. Exceptional children—Education. I. Driscoll, Maryanne, 1947–   II. Title.
LB3013.F75 1985   371.9   85-2687

ISBN: 0-8077-2771-7 (paperback)
ISBN: 0-8077-2778-4 (cloth)

Manufactured in the United States of America

90 89 88 87 86 85   1 2 3 4 5 6

This book is dedicated to our families
Chad, Meg, and Chuck
Deborah, Eden, and Mel

Contents

Preface

Teachers are under pressure to help children perform well academically. Yet discipline keeps getting mentioned as a major concern across the country. This book is designed to help teachers respond to both concerns.

The curriculum suggestions that we make throughout the book apply to special education as well as regular education teachers. The main idea is to make a better match between children's academic and personal needs and curriculum materials and activities.

We view elementary school teaching as an exciting, exquisitely humanizing experience, beyond "good" days alone. We wish to see teachers retain and refine in children an excitement about knowledge and humanity, to create learners who can become self-reflective and critical thinkers.

Pills do not exist to bring about these attributes. However, there is a body of knowledge about specific pedagogic skills that influence and develop such behaviors. This book deals with the concrete, practical application of these skills within the context of real schools at the end of the twentieth century.

Even in a classroom where you find different rates of learning and motivation, and exceptional learning needs, there are pedagogic skills that will extend the learning possibilities of all children as active experiencers of their own education. That is, there are things that a teacher can do to help make a difference in the educational experience of all children, regardless of different abilities and personal needs, while retaining the primary role of educator rather than counselor or police officer. At the same time, you ought to be able to appreciate your own work, to find personal satisfaction, and to look forward to your next encounter.

This book should be adapted by you, the reader, as you work with children, apply some of these concrete practices, and shape your own teaching life. You will be able to use experiential curricular programs to help your students be self-disciplined and self-directed.

   The recommendations we present are based upon theories that have been demonstrated to be effective and also upon what we see as the ethical responsibility of adults in schools to provide a positive, successful experience for students in an environment where sincere teaching and significant learning flourish.

   We thank Lois Patton, the acquisitions editor at Teachers College Press, for encouraging this project and Steve Carlson, Rutgers University, for helpful suggestions. To Carol Effron, who typed and served as a cheering section, we extend our all-encompassing gratitude for her devotion and professionalism.

THE SUCCESSFUL CLASSROOM
Management Strategies for Regular and Special Education Teachers

1

Giving, Taking, Sharing, and Exercising Power

INTRODUCTION: PUMPING ADRENALIN

Imagine yourself in the following fast action, high tension, adrenalin-pumping situations occurring at five-minute intervals:

Adrenalin Pump 1: You emerge in a dense jungle and suddenly find yourself being chased by a band of hostile, knife-wielding, arrow-releasing men. You are running as fast as you are able. Your heart rate increases and your throat becomes dry. You are running faster than you ever dreamed you could, but you feel as though you are in a slowed-down nightmare.

Adrenalin Pump 2: After struggling past some angry men, feeling spent, you see that flaming gasoline is quickly rolling toward your dearest friend. You muster energy that you did not imagine possible to help your friend.

Adrenalin Pump 3: Exhausted, excited to have reached your destination after overcoming countless dangers, you shine your lantern on your final step and find it to be a seething snake convention.

Adrenalin Pump 4: You are hanging on to the outside door of a rapidly moving truck while someone seated inside is trying to push you off! (Adapted from the film, *Raiders of the Lost Ark*, 1981)

Children have their adrenalin pumped every five minutes by films such as this. In contrast, in the classroom you are faced with the task of teaching them the value of silent "e" at the end of a word. Your competition for their attention, forgetting commitment for the moment, is a bit stiff. The day of the stand-up teacher-entertainer is past. Between the television and film cultures with which children come to school, it is

1

unlikely that the passive linear curriculum of directed paper-and-pencil tasks will maintain their attention or commitment.

You may even be struck by the possibility that the existing concept of schooling is obsolete. In many instances, it is. At the very least, it is artificial to toss twenty-five to thirty-five children and one adult into a finite box of space for six hours each day. Schools have therefore evolved a regimen for training children away from their natural flow of action and exploration, to on-cue responses to institutional demands. Teachers have often been teaching schooling in the name of educating. However, neither the five-minute rhythm of the thrill-based, adrenalin-pumping media nor the soporific pace of paper-and-pencil exercises and workbooks is real experience and significant learning.

Children as Experienced Learners

Children are capable of real experience. Before they arrive at school and after they depart, children show that they are incredibly able learners. They have made active choices from among materials and activities at home and outdoors. While one child studies every different insect on the way home from school, another notices and classifies cars and trucks, still another prefers spending a long time observing at a demolished building site, yet another counts the racks of clothing the men are pushing past him in his crowded garment-center neighborhood, and one child is engrossed in sharing wishes with a friend. With a range of real and imaginable choices, most children appear quite able to select a relevant pastime.

Each of these children manages to find the *time and energy* to pursue a self-selected choice. You would hardly propose that a child be scheduled to finish insects at the end of this street and begin the study of automobile traffic on the next street. You could observe the homeward-bound student of insects watching, touching, and collecting for a week or two or longer. He may well be the child who finds reading about birds interesting, who can enjoy watching and recording the development of tadpoles in a pond or aquarium, and who learns which seeds to put out for local birds. His rhythm of activity is his alone.

Experience Is Cognitive, Aesthetic, Psychomotor, and Social

The examples above indicate that children experience the world at once as cognitive, aesthetic, psychomotor, and social. They come to school having seen things that are beautiful as well as having seen things that are ugly and possibly violent. Their entire attention is devoted to solving a problem. They stand ready to repeat a skill again and again, and feel satisfied and supported in their activity. Each child needs a different amount of time to satisfy his or her repetition of mastery—whether the task is tying shoe laces, riding a bicycle, measuring liquids, writing one's name, learning to jump double dutch, or solving a three-dimensional puzzle such as a Rubik's cube.

Much of children's understanding about how things work is tied to their physical involvement, active attention, feelings of competence, and immediate appreciation of the moment itself. In short, education takes place most smoothly when children are enticed by tasks. And you, their teacher, will be in a position to make activities attractive to them.

When you consider what to teach in ways that appeal to children, you need to consider that education in school implies education of the mind. The most loving teacher who is inept at matching a task to the children's developmental capacity inflicts situations in which children may experience academic failure. And a subjective sense of failure can lead to social behavior management problems.

Skillful teachers, at any time, manage to consider children's emotional and social development. Yet the "warmth" and social sensitivity of a skilled teacher will not shelter a child from the put-down feeling of an intellectual failure. First, the teacher needs to translate adult feelings and understandings into concrete tasks that children can learn. Second, significant success will be most satisfying to the student when she has met some perceived challenge. Challenge, in this sense, involves both a risk and a perceivable chance of success—strong reasons for capturing children's attention and involvement. As you plan challenging educational activities for, and with, children, you will find that social behavior and management issues become related in ways that are helpful in children's academic learning.

CIRCULATION: THE BUFFET-STYLE SCHOOL

Children simply do not develop in the straight lines in which we imagine adults think. They do not usually choose or digest the same nourishment served to everybody at the same time. Indeed, *different children doing different things at different times can have equivalent experiences.*

In a similar way, when driving in older, European cities, the shortest distance between two points is a curve. Movement in a straight line clashes with the aesthetic of the city and its necessary system of one-way routings in narrow streets.

Some teachers have been bending and adjusting to fit children's ways of growing. Children's development meanders in curves and children are permitted to bounce against the curves of their education. Teachers that sculpt this elasticity create schools that can absorb many children who might otherwise be classified as "special" cases. In this way schools need to bend with the slower developing children as well as with those children who require extended challenges.

Consider the case of a school that serves a low-income housing project and dilapidated, privately owned houses, all set in an industrial complex. There is less open green space and more industrial soot and noise than in most other parts of this city. Rubbish is strewn over empty lots of land. Burned out and partially boarded up storefronts stand. Many heavy trucks use the area for through traffic. Transportation to the swinging life of the downtown museums, theaters, zoos, and parks means two fares and an hour's traveling.

Entry into the aged school building leaves one wondering about what possible macabre extensions of the outdoors would be found indoors. A nagging rain and overcast sky emphasize the atmosphere, blending well. When the sun shines, it is an affront, lighting up chipped bricks, cracked sections of pavements, grime-sculpted corners, and corrosion-speckled corrugated tin panels.

Many of the children wear handed-down, faded, unironed clothing from which they change into "play" clothes after school. One boy's sweater and head are covered with red lint. Several children have running sores around their mouths, some on their hands. Many heads of hair were washed perhaps a month before. One is hard put to evoke the memory of a scruffier looking lot of children.

When you enter the ancient building, designated a "priority" school, you are greeted by a dimly lit section of hall from which can be heard sounds of many children, as if at a park. The passage opens into a corridor painted in varied colors. Through the doors, you see what appears to be a well-equipped series of nursery and kindergarten rooms, with children working in small groups or alone.

Nursery-Kindergarten

Peering into a nursery-kindergarten room reveals many activities in progress. Easel painting, water measuring at the sink, playing with table-top building toys, drawing with crayons, and looking at picture books in a rug-enclosed area are located at one side of the room. The furniture subdivides the space into smaller areas reserved for these quiet activities.

On the other side of the room is a wonderland full of the sound of children's voices and activity. A teacher is bent over the sand table, talking with five children. Beyond this is an area where wooden blocks are in use. In a dramatics corner and dress-up area, children are busily occupied talking and using materials. A few children are roaming and observing.

The teacher moves away from the sand table and approaches the two children who had been roaming. The children agree when she suggests a collage activity. She helps them carry scissors, paste, and textured materials to a table in the less active section of the room. The children help themselves to materials from four shoe boxes, each of which holds materials with a different texture. The teacher cuts some cloth and tissue paper as directed by one child who cannot manage to cut them by himself. She shows him some ways to tear, fold, bunch, crush, and twist other materials so that he could work independently.

After she helps them sort misplaced materials, she walks toward the dress-up area. On the way, she stops to admire one child's perseverance with a puzzle and another child's combination of colors at the easel. She stops to ask another child who seems nearly finished with a crayon drawing what he is planning to do next. Satisfied with his response, she reaches the dress-up area and is swept up in the purchase of groceries with imaginary money and a price structure that sells apples at a dollar and cereal at a nickel.

She maintains this busy, calm pace for the better part of two hours. Four twenty-minute time samplings reveal that there are some minutes when she has contact with as many as five different children, for example:

"May I use the stapler?"
"Where should I put this?"
"Can I go to the block corner now?"
"Look!"
"Where is the fat marker?"
"Is this ready for painting?"

The children appear comfortable, reasonably happy, mostly constructively involved.

The children's comprehension vocabulary is extremely limited. The syntax of many of the three- and four-year-olds is limited to one- and two-word sentences. The faculty is aware that the children's syntax and vocabulary are restricted. The teacher is working on plans for increased verbal contacts with children through syntax model games. In addition, as she circulates from one area to another, she speaks to the children, appreciating, encouraging, questioning, and suggesting.

When she judges that the children can be expected to work independently for a few minutes, she seats herself beside three children who were dumping a mass of objects into the sides of the balance scale. She suggests a guessing game in which they sort and weigh the objects, which include bottle caps, pine cones, wood cubes, pebbles, rubber washers, spools, and red beans.

Since her assessment is correct, and she is quick to note that this is not universally true, that the dumping and giggling activity is a message for her that the children need some stimulation, the children eagerly begin to sort the materials into a set of empty coffee cans covered with colored contact paper. When they are ready, they work together, at first guessing which items would be heavier or lighter in weight and then testing their hypotheses by using the balance scale. Occasional surprises, such as a large pine cone that weighs less than a small metal bottle cap, leads to the discussion of possible reasons. The children offer alternative interpretations ranging from "because" to magic, foul play, and "It feels different."

The teacher notices which child would soon be ready for the next step, counting how many pine cones balance a bottle cap, as well as that child who needs help with sorting objects in the first place. During the year she will arrange for children to sort, classify, and compare according to color, size, shape, texture, weight, space, time, resilience, odor, change, movement, and composition. Seriation activities would follow.

This teacher appreciates that children's understandings of seriation vary and are related to the Piagetian (Piaget, 1950, 1957) concept of decentering, a process through which a young child learns to see more than his own perspective. Part of this development comes with practice and the *dissonance* between first glance observations, concrete referents, and additional experiences.

This parallels children's social development as much as it relates to their dealings with objects. Taking turns and learning to share require cognitive abilities. When adults ask a young child or a child who is developmentally delayed to wait his turn, something that some adults at checkout counters, ticket lines, and airline counters have trouble doing, we are asking him to decenter himself, to recognize that the other fellow has rights, feelings, and needs. Yet from a child's earliest days he is expected to be sociable in this cognitively demanding way. The youngest children or children who function at this level have little concept of the other person's experiencing of wants. At best, the teacher helps children with necessary language, acceptance of his feelings if not his actions, and repeated experiences. Figure 1.1 summarizes the teacher's movements that were observed. She has alternated direct teaching activities with circulating around the room. As she circulated, she engaged in a variety of teaching and management functions.

Primary

As you walk out of the kindergarten room, past two children talking over their checkerboard, hardly anyone notices because they are involved with their activities. However, when you walk up the battleship gray iron stairs past colorful murals made by children and enter the primary room, a six-year-old boy provides a hug-at-first-sight and practically drags you past four children listening to tape recorders with ear-

Figure 1.1 Nursery-Kindergarten Teacher Flow Map

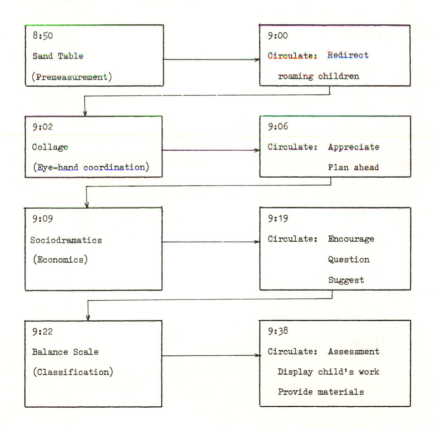

phones, two children playing with a teacher-made "Candyland" (Milton Bradley Co.) game adaptation for practice in the word families of "it" and "at," five children whose chairs face a wall in order to cut down visual distractions as they write on lined paper with pencils, a child with a ruler measuring plant sizes, six children writing responses to teacher-made computation cards using colored plastic discs, and two boys playing a teacher-made board game using dice and working in the base 4. You both join the teacher, who is seated at a round table at the far end of the room listening to a group of five children read their captions for pictures that will be made into a roller movie. Figure 1.2 summarizes the teacher's movements.

When they finish, one child goes to the office to use the primer typewriter while another goes to the easel. The teacher asks the "hugger" and three other children to remain with her for a new card game. They play "pairs" in which the cards are placed face down in random order after the words on them have been identified. Since the children had not seen the game before, the teacher takes two turns to show them how it works and to explain the need to say what you pick and replace each card in the same spot unless it is a pair.

The teacher invites you to take her place in the game. Then the teacher circulates around the room, making brief notes in a small book. She explains later that she keeps records in the book, which is indexed for each child, and she periodically checks off what materials each child uses and notes in which skills or concepts the child needs instruction. Each day she concentrates systematically on keeping track of the movements of five children although she makes notations about others. At least once each week she reviews her notes to help in planning the following week's additions and in developing longer range ideas for projects and trips.

This morning, a child had brought to school two packages of candy. The teacher asked:

Which is biggest? Which is heaviest? (Balance scale)
How many pieces are in each box?
How many shells, (peas, corks, chalks) fit around the perimeter of each box?

Although this visitor's attention span was tuned out after forty-five minutes of keeping track of this child's activity, she continued to be engrossed beyond that time. The teacher wrote a note to herself that next steps for this child might mean surveys involving seriation and other classifications, or moving beyond balancing to the use of standard weights and measures.

Figure 1.2 Primary Teacher Flow Map

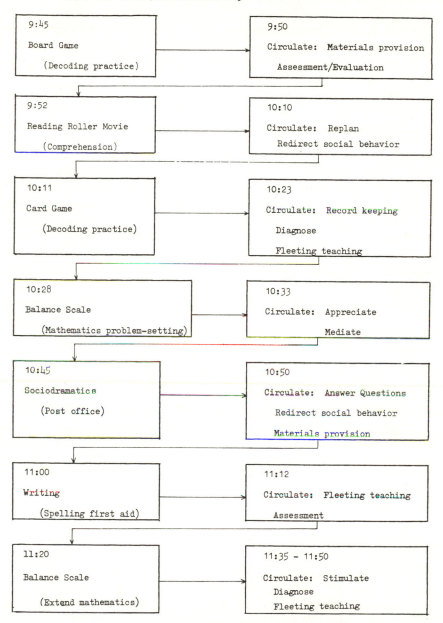

9:45	9:50
Board Game	Circulate: Materials provision
(Decoding practice)	Assessment/Evaluation

9:52	10:10
Reading Roller Movie	Circulate: Replan
(Comprehension)	Redirect social behavior

10:11	10:23
Card Game	Circulate: Record keeping
(Decoding practice)	Diagnose
	Fleeting teaching

10:28	10:33
Balance Scale	Circulate: Appreciate
(Mathematics problem-setting)	Mediate

10:45	10:50
Sociodramatic	Circulate: Answer Questions
(Post office)	Redirect social behavior
	Materials provision

11:00	11:12
Writing	Circulate: Fleeting teaching
(Spelling first aid)	Assessment

11:20	11:35 - 11:50
Balance Scale	Circulate: Stimulate
(Extend mathematics)	Diagnose
	Fleeting teaching

Circulating. The teacher appeared to follow an alternating pattern of activity. She would circulate briefly within each of the furniture subdivisions and then remain in an area with one or more children. She would listen to a child read, teach a new number concept, try to resolve a dispute, discuss plans for a new project about life in the sea, or start a new board game with a group.

After each direct teaching time she circulates around the room before beginning the next activity with another small group. As she circulates, she helps other children to replan their time as needed so that they will be involved when she needs to be doing direct instruction without distractions. Her main concern as she circulates is to help those individuals who need additional encouragement or stimulation to think of additional possibilities. She wants to be sure that minimal interruption of her direct teaching sessions will occur. She knows that when children are involved in doing purposeful learning activities, they are not likely to seek the teacher's attention when she is less readily available.

As she circulates, she is able to learn more about each child's pace, depth of involvement, and competence with each activity. She could stop for a fleeting moment of teaching, one of the most satisfying facets of her job. She could notice the child who needs help in choosing his next task and make a suggestion of what to do next, or she could attend to a child who needs to be assisted in joining another child or group in an activity. In effect, she is using the circulating opportunity to extend plans for ongoing work with children, to redirect children, to help children select and obtain needed materials, to engage in direct teaching, to bring individuals together or change group compositions in order to support positive social interaction, to enjoy and appreciate children's real accomplishments and self-directed efforts, to evaluate what they can do and how well-coordinated they are in order to diagnose their needs for possible next steps, and to record their progress on a regular basis. Figures 1.1, 1.2, and 1.3 illustrate the varying amounts of time that the teachers devote to their circulation tasks.

When you visit the seven-year-olds next door, the teacher's pattern of movement is similar. As you enter, she is just finishing a transaction at the children's post office and then suggests that you be a resource person for a group of children who are writing, in the event they ask for the spelling of a word. You notice that there seem to be a number of requests for the spelling of words with "er," "ur," "or," "ir," and "ing."

Two children line up a string of small word cards they select from a pocket chart of many words until they have a sentence. Then they copy the sentence all at once. The teacher explains that this helps them to express their idea before it is lost. In this way, they can record it before the idea is buried in the coordinating effort of the physical labor of writing.

In a nearby area are six children, using a balance scale with ounce weights. They are to find out how many green peas balance a four-ounce weight. They begin counting a pea at a time, occasionally lose count, and a child or two as well. The teacher sits down with the group and helps them to translate counting into weighing and multiplying. As she interacts with them, the original group grows to seven involved children. Six additional "observing" children gather around the table.

They continue together with the teacher alternately circulating around the room—to appreciate, answer questions, and redirect other children—and sitting with this group during a thirty-five minute period. They dissect the numbers at various points and put them back together again. They move on to replace the peas with round blocks and the four-ounce weights are replaced with eight-ounce weights. Then they compute how many blocks there are in a pound.

Each time she moves around the room, the teacher suggests a new activity to three children who appear to be engrossed in conversation. Each time they follow her suggestion briefly. In turn, they paint, converse, do needlework, converse, do woodwork, and relapse into their conversation. Finally, they become involved for a long period in planning a play, writing out parts, and measuring for costumes. When asked about this group, the teacher shared her philosophy that it is sometimes difficult for an observer to see purpose in continually resurgent gossip, even though Piaget et al. (1965) and other developmentalists (Isaacs, 1930) explain that interaction and dialogue with one's peer group are necessary contributions to intellectual development and self-awareness.

In terms of developing a personal teaching style, another teacher might have chosen to separate these children sooner than took place here, in order to help them remain engaged in a purposeful learning activity. The issue of what makes an activity purposeful is an important one. It is based on the teacher's philosophy, the level of the child's development, and the nature of the program goals, which do change from time to time.

Occasional children, and each child on occasion, may wander, apparently uninvolved in school activity. This situation could resemble the perpetual-motion-prolific artist who suddenly appears to have retired from continual production and motion. This artist could put into words what the child is telling us by his behavior. In effect, "Sometimes I have to take the time to absorb, assimilate, and accumulate new experiences and feelings before I can put them into any form." In fact, the shape of such forms, whether they are written, built, or painted, and the child's social behavior have served as the teacher's means for assessing children's understandings.

It is possible that the wandering child needs more attention from his teacher to help him find a fitting activity. Undoubtedly some children require differing degrees of direction and structure, and teachers who are more and less able to mesh accordingly. There is no universal prescription. Each teacher or group will develop a unique style. Chapters 5 and 6 suggest some alternative ways in which teachers structure learning environments.

It is relevant to weigh the emphasis on individualized and small group instruction and activity against conventional instruction. Surely, if children are more passively occupied with attending all together to a "teacher-entertainer," one cannot as easily evaluate how many children are attending and absorbing and how many have vacated their bodies. Did you ever intentionally look out the window when you knew the answer, so that the teacher would ask you to recite—and look interested when your mind was elsewhere?

Intermediate

Upon entering the room used by the eleven-year-olds, there appeared to be spaces set apart for writing, reading, science and mathematics work, collaborative social studies and art constructions, as well as a computer center at which six children were sharing four machines. The teacher finished showing eight children in the mathematics area how to use some materials for calculations with fractions and left them solving problems independently, occasionally referring to some subdivided wooden discs. As she moved slowly past the computer area, one child asked her how to program a diagonal. The teacher asked in turn:

What have you tried already?
What happened?
What did you do that was similar last week?
How are they different?
When you move your body in that way, how is it similar? Different?
What could be a first step that you have not tried before?

The teacher did not provide "the correct" answer but did enter into the process of solving the problem as the other children in the area converged around them to see what would happen and to discuss alternatives. When the group had settled into their own programs with some questions from the teacher, individual requests to show what they were doing, and appreciation of their efforts, the teacher moved to look over the shoulders of children who were writing individually. She passed through the reading section, and sat briefly with a youngster who was working on sorting the spelling patterns of suffixes.

The teacher was last seen hearing the latest work of six children who were writing a play about the inhabitants of a New England town during the Civil War. In order to write their play, the children needed to refer to many books of the period, fiction and nonfiction, as well as to a historical road map and some documents collected in the "Jackdaw" series (Grossman Publishers, 1966). The teacher took note of the *listening skills* of the playwriting group: "You're picking up on one another's interpretations. Even grownups have trouble listening that carefully. Good for you!"

As she circulated, the teacher commented with pleasure to individual children for demonstrating

Progress: "These are really complex math problems. Remember how difficult it was when we began to work with fractions? You've come a long way."

Perseverance: "Nobody finds editing smooth and easy. You've really turned around that report. It's so much clearer now that you've spent the time."

Quiet concentration: "You were so involved in your book that you wouldn't have been able to see Darth Vader at the window— even if he had come. Impressive concentration, I'd say! Keep it up."

When she saw an unhappy looking girl begin to fidget with her fractions problems, the teacher stopped to see where the child's upset originated. When it was clear that the child needed help, the teacher offered it and suggested that she might continue the work then or later. The child noted that she would prefer to work on a chart later and would complete the problems now. Figure 1.3 summarizes the teacher's movements.

OPTIONS: PROVIDING APPROPRIATE CHOICES

The children and teachers who were visited in the inner city school appeared able to digest their buffet. That is, children made choices that were preselected by the teacher. In turn, the teacher helped them to

Figure 1.3   Intermediate Teacher Flow Map

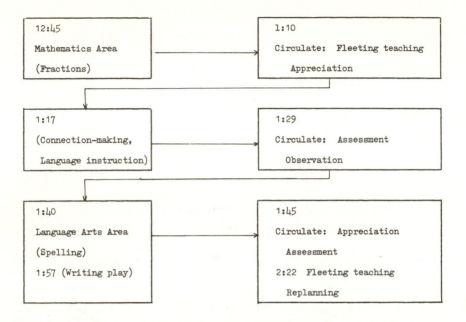

select those things they needed as well as those things they wanted. Inasmuch as the children had sufficient opportunities to make choices of their own, of which they were capable, they were more open to accepting the teacher's suggestions.

We would expect that not all options are equally valuable for different children at a particular time. It is possible that there are points of negotiating when a child's wants may exceed her needs. There are moments when sharing limited resources means that a child may need to postpone or substitute an activity.

The important issue is that your own observations would be borne out by varied literature, which indicates that self-selected activity is more likely to yield effective participation and extended time on-task (Cazden, 1972; Montessori, 1965; Zentall, 1975).

However, when a two-year-old is whining in the afternoon without apparent cause, it is pointless for an adult to ask, "Do you want to take a nap, dear?" The two-year-old is probably not able to cope with the question. Furthermore, regardless of a child's answer to a yes-no type of question, if the adult has made a reasoned decision and is willing to accept only one answer, then it seems dishonest to ask the question in the first place.

The nature of choices in school can be viewed against this framework since it is a flexible, interactive framework. That is, given the range of possible adult styles and children's styles, adults can frame the kinds of questions about choices, and the numbers of choices, with which they can abide.

The teacher provides these choices in the form of activity options available to all, some, or one child at any time. In one instance, a teacher circulating in a room asks a child, "*What* are you planning to do when you complete your story?" knowing that this child can independently answer that question. In another case, "Will you begin your survey *or* start your science project when you finish in the dramatics corner?" is the question he asks of a child who could use more involvement with construction materials. In yet another case, the teacher says, "When you finish the puzzle, please come to the measuring corner. I want to begin a new activity with you." Or, "When you finish this, bring it to me so that we can discuss it." If the child offers another reasonable suggestion, the teacher accepts it and can reschedule him for the measuring activity: "All right, we can do it first thing after lunch."

On one level, the number of choices available to a child is tempered by the teacher's judgment at that moment in relation to a particular child. Children frequently create relevant choices. At another level, the number of different activity possibilities occurring at the same time varies from teacher to teacher and at different times during the day.

A large-group planning session, discussion, story telling, or performance represents a single activity. There may be a child or two who are not able to concentrate during a large-group activity or who are not able to participate in a particular activity without disrupting other children. In this case, other quiet activities are planned *in advance* with the individual children who need this attention. By planning in a positive manner for these special situations beforehand, the group's time is protected and the individual child's right to dignified treatment is respected.

Options, therefore, vary across a wide span of possibilities. In this sense, there is a "next step" of options possible for different children at different times as well as for a teacher, beginning with any number of activity choices and expanding from there as he or she feels able. There is no single ideal image. Rather, there are as many as there are practitioners.

A central consideration in deciding how many different activity options a teacher can plan relates to the children's ability to make a real choice. It is worth underscoring that *a real choice is an informed choice*.

A real choice involves some degree of challenge and the expectation that children can feel involved in the activity. In addition, the teacher can recognize and provide for legitimate choices wherein children might structure an activity or make a discovery that the teacher had not previously discovered.

While it is exciting when an activity or material offers a range of possible interpretations, offerings must be appropriate to the abilities of children. When children use their perceptual powers to move outside a teacher's range of expectancies, the teacher's franchise is extended rather than diminished. Insights can be gained by the teacher to suggest ideas for additional planning and support for children's imaginativeness.

RHYTHM: SELF-PACING AND RECYCLING

When people say that children have short attention spans, we must ask, "To what?" Certainly, the seven-year-old who was measuring for more than forty-five minutes had a long attention span. She was involved actively in her work. While we would hardly expect that a seven-year-old would engage in five successive forty-five minute sedentary projects, we would respect her need to complete an engrossing learning activity.

On the other hand, children whose own rhythm is interrupted, who are required to change frequently from one activity to another before they are ready, may learn not to invest their energy in depth. They are children whose self-direction is undermined and whose attention is, at best, polite. In a more honest expression of their feelings, they act distracted, or at worst, destructive. A teacher who arbitrarily changes activities for everybody by the clock encourages distractability. Rather, it is important to alternate sedentary and active pastimes within a flexible format.

When each child feels the power to select an activity and pursue it for a satisfying amount of time, she feels a greater sense of responsibility for the outcome of the activity. In turn, the teacher who provides for some long blocks of time each day supports scholarship. Such longer intervals allow the flexibility to plan for the children who need activities broken down into shorter benchmarks quite as well as for those children who can organize their own time effectively. Children can then extend their attention span as they find meaning in their occupations.

Meaning involves a changing commitment. Meaning moves a concrete situation beyond itself. Therefore, beyond looking at choices of activities to offer children, teachers need to consider a child's perceptions of those options that are worth his or her investment of time and energy. Observing how children spend their self-selected time or asking a child for a suggestion among choices is useful.

Self-Pacing

The teacher, planning with children, can extend possibilities for the practice of needed tool skills while respecting the kind of self-pacing children are capable of. In short, there is a clear place for direct instruction of small groups and individuals through the use of alternative strategies.

For example, if a child had not signed up for individual reading with the teacher, he might be asked to opt for "either-or" time, or "now-or-later today." During a planning session, the teacher could easily ask several children to start their activity time with the teacher if the need for a particular skill was evident in their performance.

In traditional settings, children usually follow the teacher's pace. That is, children most frequently respond to the teacher's soliciting actions (Bellack, Kliebard, Hyman, & Smith, 1966). This writer's observations in more decentralized settings contrasts with the Bellack et al. study of usual settings, and indicates that the children approach the teacher much more than in traditional settings and ask many more questions of the teacher. A related observation is that the teacher's presence in an area is sufficient to draw children to the area. Serbin (1978) documents similar teacher influence in a situation where children can choose where they will work.

Self-pacing means that children feel relatively free to move from one area to another as needed. The degree of movement does reflect teacher style and personality. In order for such movement to work effectively in the artificially confining space of a classroom, teachers need to learn and anticipate certain behaviors.

The teacher's task is to anticipate children's needs or adapt to them by setting materials in or near the area where they will be used. Children should know where to use materials, thereby cutting down unnecessary traffic. Moreover, when the teacher sets out priority materials before the children arrive, he creates a smooth transition and supports concentration.

The earliest weeks of the school year are an important time in which to establish where things are used and how they are treated when children have finished with them. During this time the teacher is constantly circulating, appreciating focused efforts, supporting children's self-direction, and constantly, repeatedly, sharing the question that children need to learn to ask themselves: "What are you going to do when you put away these things or finish this project?"

Self-pacing is supported by the internalization of this question *coupled with* the presence of stimulating activities. Stimulating activities exist in the child's perceptions rather than as absolute attributes of the activity. One teacher of twelve-year-olds found that a solubility study group that nobody chose to attend had a waiting list several weeks later. She had retitled the activity "Mysterious Potions" and used an ambiguous picture to identify the sign-up sheet. A modest merchandising success, the activity drew many children over a period of time and stimulated exciting hypothesizing.

The content of "relevant choices" is a pivotal variable if we expect children to stay with an independent activity. In the early weeks, when a teacher and children are learning how to interact with one another, it is useful to plan for those independent activities that require minimal teacher monitoring and minimal direct instruction. In this way, the teacher can circulate and reinforce productive behavior. As children gain self-direction in choosing and pacing, the teacher adds options that may require increasing teacher involvement, such as playing a game with more complex moves or providing a needed tool skill.

Some teachers who were newcomers to an integrated activity period began with a *daily* hour during which they focused on traffic management, organization, ongoing short-range planning, and training children for self-direction. There is growing evidence that developing a foundation of classroom routines is a necessary first step in effective classroom management (Weber, Roff, Crawford, & Robinson, 1983, p. 30). When children have been exposed to these consistent, repeated guidelines coupled with a range of relevant choices, several teachers in inner-city settings have observed a marked decrease in aggressive behavior and random movement. These observations are supported by research reviews (Charles, 1983; Weber et al., 1983). At the same time, we must underscore the importance of regularly available activity periods to avoid the kind of starved response that leads children to gorge themselves. Such gorging is manifested by short attention spans as children rush to taste rare opportunities.

The teacher has more opportunity for direct instruction of small groups when the bulk of the remaining group is actively involved in planning together for, and then engaging in, other activities independently. Nevertheless, a particular group of children can become saturated by the demands of activities and materials on two levels.

Just as a plant can be overwatered, so can children be overstimulated by too many choices for which they are unprepared. Unfortunately, some fearful teachers may use such awareness as an excuse for imposing whole-group action. Rather, there may be merely a need for reducing the options by a single, particular activity, or there may be a particular independent activity offered at the same time as another one which requires frequent monitoring by the teacher. Sometimes this "saturation effect" can be alleviated by reducing by one or two children the number who may engage simultaneously in a particular activity, or it may be that a particular child needs to be redirected away from the group.

Recycling Materials and Concepts

Another consideration with reference to saturating a child's environment resides in how long a particular material will be available for children to use. In one study a kind of wave motion was observed when a new material was added (Fromberg, 1965, pp. 100ff.). The first wave consisted of a small group of more assertive children who monopolized the material intermittently for a week or two and then gave it only cursory attention. The second wave consisted of a somewhat less assertive group who appeared to alternate with the first group. These children were followed by individuals who had observed at a distance for a few days until the first two waves had receded. After they completed a kind of "circuit of safety," they settled with the material.

A general pattern seems to be that individuals actively use the materials, then intermittently use them, and then give the objects only cursory attention—until they rediscover them some weeks or months later. It is at the cursory attention point in the use of materials that they may be removed as an option because they are no longer relevant. However, when they are made available six or eight weeks later, possibly with or without added complexity, these same materials are likely to become relevant again. Such activities as open-ended science materials, construction devices, art media, pets, and games lend themselves to this recycling.

New concepts can also be recycled three to six weeks after their introduction. For example, a group of eight-year-olds had been taught about centrifugal force using many concrete materials that kept the entire class involved for twenty-five minutes. However, the teacher felt very frustrated at the end of the lesson. She was not at all clear that the children learned any of the concepts that she had intended. A classroom observer commented that the children in the group seemed to be more careful observers than at an earlier activity. They seemed more able to challenge the observations of others and to try out some explanations for events.

Since the children seemed to need more time to explore the materials, the teacher devoted direct instruction during the following three weeks to other things, leaving the materials available. When she brought up the subject three weeks later, she was surprised that the children seemed to have made quite a number of fresh observations and associations. They seemed to have learned more tacitly during the intervening period.

This teacher's observations are similar to the memory studies done by Luria (1968) and Piaget, Sinclair, and Bliss (Piaget & Inhelder, 1969), using a series of graduated sticks. One week after seeing the sticks, the children made drawings that showed what they understood about what they had seen. Six months later, not having seen the model again, "80 percent of the cases" responded with "slightly superior" recall. (Piaget & Inhelder, 1969, p. 82). Apparently, once individuals perceive something, it remains with them. Over time, the perceived material becomes tied to other experiences. Therefore, when the eight-year-olds who had explored centrifugal force returned several weeks later, their readiness had grown to become "more than the sum of its parts."

Therefore, beyond planning for variable pacing and long time blocks for independent work, scholarship is strengthened when materials and concepts are recycled from time to time. As recycling occurs, children have a chance to have fresh social contacts with each other. When social contacts occur, they can be a vital educational force. It helps a teacher to be aware of what impact various social actions and inactions can have on children's self-concepts and subsequent academic work.

FEELINGS: LEGITIMATE SOCIALIZATION

"Richie is a cry-baby. Richie is a cry-baby." Two eight-year-old boys are chanting, pointing at Richie, whose distress deepens. Richie runs into his house, tears streaming, trying to suppress his sobs, ashamed. The sting of his skinned knees has been pushed aside by the greater pain of ridicule.

Each of us has been Richie and each of us has seen Richie. Children learn the lesson very early. Hide your feelings. Deny your feelings. Control your anger. Don't laugh so loud or giggle so much. What *can* a child do?

One adult, observing a five-year-old's jealousy over a new baby, was sensitive to her feelings and gave her a large inflatable frog as a punching bag:

> TEACHER: Now, Peggy, I see you feel it's hard to have a new baby. When you feel like hitting the baby, you can hit Big Frog instead.
>
> PEGGY: Oh, but I *like* Big Frog!

Fortunately, the teacher was able to give Peggy snap-apart blocks, clay, and special moments of individual attention threaded through the day. Her parents also found ways for Peggy to provide real help around the house, such as using a magnet to help her mother collect thumb tacks that had fallen on the floor, and holding the hose while her parents washed the car. In short, Peggy was distracted by responsibilities and activities that had prestige in the child's culture and with which she could feel successful.

Obvious material damage to limb and property rates more active attention in many settings than does damage to feelings. When ten-year-old Hetty quietly tells each smaller child individually that she will beat him up, that he is a liar, or that he is ugly, and boasts about her out-of-school possessions and activities, little notice is taken. However, when she takes a child's plastic bracelet or extorts a dime in exchange for avoiding harassment, adults take notice.

It is probably a useful clue that Hetty is having difficulty reading. She needs individual instruction. In addition, she needs other ways in which she can feel competent. Her teacher provided her with a special pocket folder in which she could store her own statements that had been copied with the help of an older child-tutor. As this folder fills, Hetty can see concrete progress. Feeding and weighing the class guinea pig and white mice—a prestigious task in this group—are her jobs for this week. The teacher makes special note every few minutes to let Hetty know by a few words or a smile and nod when he sees her concentrating on her work or being helpful.

However, when she slips into her attention-getting behaviors, the teacher works at ignoring her behavior while giving the other children who are on-task more positive appreciation. At the first sign of Hetty's return to acceptable behavior, the teacher resumes the appreciation of her work. The technique of teacher approval and selective ignoring has been found to be effective in a variety of school settings (O'Leary & O'Leary, 1977). The technique is based on the principle of positive reinforcement (see Rimm & Masters, 1979), which is discussed at length in chapter 4.

While these are beginning steps that may need to be followed by more specialized counseling, it is important to avoid making Hetty a scapegoat. Scapegoating can happen all too easily, when an exasperated teacher repeatedly reprimands the same child in front of others. It is too simple for the children to project their own inadequacies onto the target child. It is much more effective to take aside an offender and briefly discuss her feelings, her rights, and the feelings and rights of others. It also helps, instead of outrage, to find out both sides of an issue before assuming that the repeating offender is guilty.

> TEACHER: Oh, Chris won't let you use the pendulums? Why do you
>   think she feels that way?
> JAN: I don't know.
> CHRIS: I was working there first and she came over and she just
>   changed it.
> JAN: You're selfish!
> TEACHER: You feel you want to use the pendulum too, and Chris
>   feels that she worked to build something and wants it to stay that
>   way. What are some things you can do so that both of you can be
>   happy?

When the teacher helps each child's feelings to be stated, both children feel accepted. When the teacher asks them for some solutions she is suggesting that there may be more than one way to resolve the dispute. She is also suggesting that they are capable of being responsible for working out problems. With repeated practice and help from the teacher, both children may develop a habit of seeking alternate solutions.

In addition, by reserving judgment, the teacher avoids falling into the trap of wrongly decoding, "I was using it first." That simple statement might also mean, "I had it first—when she turned her head for an instant," or "I taunted her into enough anger to ruin my construction." Similar arguments about sharing materials arise among all groups of children and will be discussed in chapter 2.

At best, teachers can deal in educated guesses concerning a child's sense of self-confidence while reserving judgment during a dispute. Teachers who provide a positive, accepting attitude avoid labelling children. They recognize that each of us tries to sustain our own image of ourselves. Lecky (1969) proposes a theory of self-concept based on "self-consistency." That is, a person is likely to act according to his self-picture even if it is false, unhealthy, or hurtful to do so. Each child sees himself selectively and accepts or rejects an action based upon how he sees himself.

Thus, if the teacher provides a child with, or implies, a label or attitude of "slow" or "clumsy" or "thief" or "immature" or "aggressive," a child will frequently manage to live up to the appraisal. Then, problems multiply. The central issue in teaching is that a child needs to feel powerful, competent. When he feels inadequate, problems such as fighting, destructiveness, withdrawal, inattention, fear, and unhappiness usually arise.

The core issue in helping children to cope with their feelings about themselves can be distilled to two strong provisions. The teacher needs to (1) accept the child's feelings and (2) provide the child with responsibilities.

Self-pacing by children, discussed above, is one such responsibility upon which many teachers have come to depend. Some teachers need to overcome the traditional fear of moving children. Self-pacing does affect social contacts because children will be moving about the room from time to time.

Legitimate opportunities for children to speak with one another can be built into activities and materials such as constructions, peer-assisted instruction, cooperative measurement projects, board and card game playing, creative dramatics, play writing, and sharing riddles and jokes.

When a teacher has organized relevant activity options and has supported self-direction consistently, then peer interaction becomes the powerful educative force that such developmentalists as Piaget recognize as important.

The Group as an Agent of Change

When we think of children in a group influencing each other, we often think first—with a mixture of aversion and fascination—of such occurrences as irrepressible giggling, or follow-the-leader conspiracies every time the teacher's back is turned, as well as the more frightening threat of mob violence. Such events testify to the power of the group being greater than that of individual members.

Charles (1983) cites research in which teachers suggest that unacceptable social behavior is so disruptive as to consume up to 50 percent of instructional time. In their responses, teachers felt that 80 percent of classroom management problems was caused by children talking to their neighbors and most of the remaining 20 percent of other problems was caused by children walking about the room without permission.

In classrooms where whole-group and large-group instruction is practiced, such behaviors have occurred. They can grow from the influence of an overstimulated or understimulated child quite as much as from a few children whose defensive pattern includes acting-out behavior. However, the likelihood of group upheaval is minimized when a classroom is organized around smaller units of contact and smaller areas for communication.

Every teacher at some time is going to miss the mark with a child or a small group in relation to activity. However, if there are some elastic procedures of options and self-pacing built into the classroom structure, such natural misjudgments can be contained.

Part of the process of group change relates to leadership styles among the children as well as the teacher. A first step takes place when the teacher shares with the children the process of planning activities by *sharing the problem* to be solved, the question that needs group response, or the procedure that needs group commitment.

When a subgroup of a sixth-grade class came to their teacher, complaining about the boring music teacher, she asked them what would wake them up and make them more active participants. The children said they wanted more say in what songs they should sing and more say about things that were on their minds during the music "appreciation" discussions.

Their teacher suggested that they plan what they could bring to the music class and to share that with the music teacher. Afterward, they met with the music teacher to discuss their feelings and suggestions for student presentations. He agreed to try some of their presentations and suggestions for songs. When the children had the experience of trying to keep the discussion going during their own presentations, they gained, in turn, a sense of the music teacher's experience in keeping the class's attention. As they shared ownership of the problems, they began to share responsibility. A few weeks later, the music teacher commented with pleasure to the classroom teacher about this sixth-grade class, wondering what was turning around the children (Charles L. Gleason, personal communication, 1982).

Another step in turning group activity toward social ends lies in helping children experience collaborative project development and presentation to a larger group. Just as the music class presenters gained ownership of class time by planning and presenting their projects, other children have had similar experiences in the areas of language arts, the sciences, creative arts, and the social sciences. The subgroup of presenters builds an internal sense of belonging and camaraderie. There are even studies that document higher achievement among children who had opportunities to talk with one another about school-related work (Cobb, 1972).

As children work together to prepare presentations, they have a chance to model for one another the subprocedures of their work, sometimes in ways that an adult teacher might have overlooked or excluded. A related teaching approach has been used successfully with a fourth-grade class studying science. The teacher taught a science lesson to about one-third of the group each week. The subgroup of children became peer disseminators for the other students in the class. Each time, the teacher worked with a different group of children. Between times, she worked with the entire group, using questioning, to explore ways to apply their learnings from the smaller settings (Elizabeth Meng, personal communication, 1981).

In the course of being peer disseminators, children used some of the techniques that the teacher had modeled. In other settings, children were able to model immediate positive feedback for those children who were concentrating on their work. Rather than blaming or berating another child for off-task behavior, one child was able to share his feelings by saying, "When you do that, I can't think and I feel uncomfortable." On earlier occasions, the teacher typically used that wording. Additional ways in which a teacher can influence positive leadership styles that involve cooperation, appreciation of differences, and caring will be elaborated in chapter 3.

SUMMARY

This chapter makes the point that even the youngest children and children with developmental delays are capable of pursuing self-selected, purposeful learning activities at their own levels of development. We take the position that every group is somewhat heterogeneous and that this can be conducive to learning.

The medium of a simulated visit to an inner city school presents the pattern of teachers who alternate direct teaching of small groups with circulating for many valuable program and behavior-management purposes. Circulation activities allow teachers to assume many roles during a school day. As teachers coordinate options and manage pacing, they assume the following roles:

1. Data Collector and Diagnostician
    Observing: Looking at children systematically, watching progress, plateaus, and pitfalls.
    Assessing and evaluating children's products: What has been mastered? What needs more time?
    Diagnosing: Observing children's efforts and accomplishments to determine readiness for next steps or areas needing more direct instruction.

2. Activity Guide and Traffic Manager

Extending plans and planning: Depending upon a child's progress, deepening task involvement or moving in another direction.

Redirecting children: Suggesting different activities to a child who has completed a task or who needs a change of focus.

Obtaining materials: Making sure that materials are accessible where possible and retrieving them when necessary.

Fleeting teaching: Responding to the teachable moment.

3. Matchmaker and Facilitator

Supporting positive social interaction: Planning for cooperative learning.

Enjoying and appreciating: Building up accomplishments and efforts through positive signals.

Mediating: Helping children take responsibility for their own actions.

4. Catalyst for Information Discovery and Retrieval

Questioning: Choosing questions that extend children's thinking and connection making.

Answering questions: Providing answers that help children extend their own thinking and connection-making possibilities.

Suggesting: Planning suggestions that encourage children to make informed choices.

In order to plan, organize, and schedule activities that can meet the diverse needs of children several factors were discussed:

Options: How many? When? For whom?
Pacing: How long? When? For whom?
Socialization: When? For whom? How to assist learning?

We recommend that teachers:

Look at purposes for which they are organizing groups in order to plan
Arrange for flexible scheduling
Alternate circulating and planned direct instruction of groups
Alternate active and sedentary activities
Provide children with cooperative as well as individual activities
Consider that different children doing different things at different times can have equivalent experiences.

We encourage you to draw from various program sources that are consistent with your concept of human nature.

CONCLUSIONS AND REFLECTIONS

You may not have been able to see or hear it as you read the preceding pages, but the children in these classrooms were moving purposefully to obtain materials, to use materials, or to approach another child. In turn, children who were seated next to each other, in the smaller spaces, were conversing from time to time about their work. They would show a finding, share an exciting or funny line in a book, or show proudly what they had done. There was a civilized buzz of conversation much of the time as the teacher worked with small groups and circulated around the room.

During infrequent whole-group activities, children were reasonably able to hear out one another and listen to the teacher. Nevertheless, there were occasional excited outbursts during group lessons as well as independent work times. Such occasional outbursts are natural to any group. When you receive them with humor, and with an appreciation of children's active involvement and interest, you send children the message that academic work can be satisfying, enjoyable, and comradely.

If you try to avoid such natural enthusiasm or squelch the buzz of conversation, you are really moving against the social nature of human beings and losing an important social lever, since the group can be an important agent of change. If most children are actively involved in learning and like their work much of the time, then the occasional disturbance is less likely to pull them off-task. If the work is dull paper-and-pencil programming and largely whole-group instruction, with the teacher repeatedly telling children to "be quiet, be still, get to work," then it gives the class clown more power to distract.

Successful classroom management is the ongoing collaboration between teacher and children in a learning environment that results in academic progress and civilized social behavior. Teachers have found ways to help develop self-direction, independence, and responsibility in children using successful classroom management methods. It is to these methods and techniques that we turn in chapter 2. As we do so, it is worthwhile to keep in mind philosopher John Macmurray's observation: "All meaningful knowledge is for the sake of action, and all meaningful action for the sake of friendship" (1969, p. 15).

QUESTIONS TO CONSIDER

1. What is your personal hierarchy of purposeful activities in your classroom?

2. What activities are so important that everybody should have a chance to do them?
3. Select one concept that you have taught to a group of children this week. What are the other ways that the same concept can be acquired using different activities?
4. Compare children's self-selected as opposed to teacher-assigned tasks for time on task. What types of tasks result in longer periods of time on task?
5. How does your classroom compare with the six recommendations summarized above?

2

Developing Independence
and Responsibility in Children

Before the children arrived on Monday morning, the prekindergarten teachers entered their classrooms and found a shambles set off by paint-splattered walls. The file cabinets had been wrenched open and white glue draped across the file folders. Heads of toys had been ripped off and thrown about. Torn books had been urinated upon. The pencil sharpener had been stuffed with a rotten egg, which wasn't discovered for several weeks in spite of its atrocious odor (Joyce McGinn & Fredda Lynn, personal communication, 1975).

While the teachers recognized that such violence by preadolescents grew out of a sense of powerlessness, the cleanup process was still odious. After the cleanup, these teachers discussed together how they might support the sense of power and mastery that children need to have in order to build a foundation of inner controls. If they could help build children's inner controls and sense of power while they were younger, perhaps the children would have fewer reasons to be destructive.

They knew about research supporting the notion that children who have had reasonable options and early independence were less destructive when adults left a room (Martin, 1975). Self-directed children were able to see themselves becoming more responsible for their own behavior. They did not need to look ahead toward a sense of nothingness, of anxiety, of being out of control.

WHOLE-GROUP VERSUS SMALL-GROUP INSTRUCTION

Children have a greater sense of control and personal power when they feel that they can choose, and when they can feel successful. Such a sense of accomplishment is more likely when small-group instruction rather than whole-group instruction takes place. When you try to teach a concept to an entire class at one time, planning tends to fall somewhere in the middle of group ability, at some common denominator. However, there may be many children for whom it is too simple or too complex. Beyond politeness—perhaps behind politeness—may lie anxiety and boredom.

For example, some teachers of six-year-olds frequently insist that whole-group instruction is essential for teaching the children to write the letters of the alphabet. Since some children have already done quite a bit of copying and some writing from the ages of four or five years, they might be better off using their time for more productive, satisfying purposes. For those children who do not yet have the necessary coordination to write letters, seeing their peers writing can afford a devastating comparison and inhibit their ability to take risks. However, if the teacher provides some opportunities for children to write their names, copy their own dictated poetry or shopping lists or labels or so forth, he can easily see who needs additional help in certain skills and group these children for these purposes.

In a similar way, teachers often feel that the entire group should be taught a new mathematical procedure together. For example, in one classroom when all the nine-year-olds were taught long division together, eight of the children who were still shaky about place value experienced a snowball effect of defeat. Had their teacher planned for both those children who were shaky about place values as well as for those who were ready to move on, there might have been fewer disruptions. Those who needed more work might have been given more time with bean sticks, base 10 blocks, and chip-trading games before having been expected to apply the prerequisite knowledge of place value to the long division. While these children are using supplementary materials with task cards, the teacher can spend five to ten minutes in direct instruction with the other children who are ready for the next step.

If you want to keep the whole group occupied at the same time, you will have to be a great, successful entertainer. A successful entertainer has to change frequently from one activity to another in order to keep the audience's attention.

The problem that develops in learning is that many children need time to get involved in an activity and to reflect on it. These children may become confused when the teacher-entertainer moves on to yet another activity before they had a chance to get involved in, or complete, an earlier activity.

In every classroom there is really only a very small group of "antsy" children, perhaps two to four who need special planning. The main group basically knows what to do when a well-organized foundation has been laid early in the school year. When teachers insist on whole-group attention, they play into the weakness of the more active, volatile children, giving them lots of opportunities for negative attention and negative control over the time of the main group.

When you plan for more small-group instruction time, you can attend more evenly to the learning needs of more children. It may even be helpful to plan a day that you spend mostly in direct instruction and circulation between small groups and some individuals.

Another thing to consider when trying to teach large groups over long periods of time is that young bodies simply need to move. Even as adults, we need to move and have learned to socialize or institutionalize this need. When we sit at lectures, we cross and recross our legs, alternate hands on chins, adjust glasses, brush moustaches, press fingers, and shift our weight from time to time.

Even when the well-meaning teacher-entertainer changes scene and tempo every ten or fifteen minutes, children may receive a message that says, "It really does not pay to invest yourself in anything that is going on because it will soon change." In this sense, frequent changes of activity undercut real scholarship and commitment. Therefore, it is important to keep large-group instruction to a minimum and to balance it carefully with small-group instruction, teacher circulation, independent work, and more teacher circulation.

Nevertheless, there are a number of opportunities for large groups to be together within school settings. Trips outside the group's assigned space, discussions concerning social and political issues, values discussions, films, dramatizations, meetings with resource people, storytelling, movement or music activities, sharing science findings, parties, and other timely events are possibilities.

OWNERSHIP: SCHEDULES AND ROUTINES

An entire group can plan together for the use of time and resources. Intermediate age children need less frequent replanning on an individualized basis than do primary age children. Sometimes, planning together for the kinds of activities in which to engage can take place at the end of a major activity period. Teacher and children can look together at how individuals used their time. The beginning of the next activity period can be a time in which children can commit themselves to begin a particular task. When children make the commitment, they are likely to experience a sense of ownership for that activity. We can see some ways in which planning takes place by observing the scheduling process of a group of eight-year-olds after two months of working together.

Come inside the teacher's head as she thinks ahead during the tenth week of the school year. The interest centers already contain a range of options for different children. There are two new biographies of famous women in the library corner, standing open in the middle of the round table. One is of Elizabeth Garrett, England's first woman physician.

The other is of Marie Curie, with three offerings by authors who address different reading abilities (Henriod, 1970; Henry, 1966; McKown, 1971). In this way, children of different reading abilities can share a common strand of content. Other content areas with books written at different reading abilities are sports (Brewster, 1963; Burchard, 1975; Olson, 1974; Sullivan, 1968) and motors (Bendick, 1971; Chapman, 1974; Zim, 1953; Meyer, 1962). Generally, the teacher also planned for new concepts to be available by supplying some books that were at an easier reading range than would be the case for fictional offerings. When comprehension is the main purpose of reading nonfiction material, it makes sense to provide material at a somewhat easier level of decoding. In that way, the decoding level would not be an impediment to understanding.

Perhaps those children who had been working on the automobile motor donated by a neighborhood mechanic could record their wrench and screwdriver activities. They can read in order to add labels to the motor parts, and to develop a large illustrated class chart, as well as produce some personal writing. Two children ask to take the books and writing materials to the "motor corner." The teacher asks, "Who else would like to work with them on doing a chart?" Three children raise their hands and the teacher adds their names to the chalkboard on which she had listed some options *before* the children arrived. She records each child's choice for a beginning activity.

Schedules

When the Cuisenaire rods were discussed, the teacher said, "Today I would like Larry, Meg, Ned, and Ollie to begin with me."

NED: Will I have time to go back to my writing this morning? I want to start drawing for my horse story, too.
TEACHER: You'll have time for it afterwards. Besides, I've missed doing numbers with you lately and I want to show you some new things.
NED: (hesitantly nods agreement)

TEACHER: We have a measuring wheel this week which two people can use in the hallways and gym with these question cards. . . . All right, Jan and Ken. Syl, you can use it when they finish.

SYL: Can I go to the mystery table today?

TEACHER: (nods) Who else would like to? Stan? All right. Anybody else?

UNA: I want to sign up for the easel first. I'd like to try that new green paint and the thin brushes.

EDEN: What's at the mystery table anyway?

TEACHER: What did you want to do first today?

EDEN: I'm finishing a story about Tufty, my guinea pig, and his adventures when he gets out of his cage. If it's a book about animals, I would go to the mystery table. (A few children speak quietly.)

TEACHER: Remember about the mystery table. You take your chances, using the timer at a ten-minute minimum setting if you start there. You can go later if you prefer.

EDEN: Maybe later.

TEACHER: Who else will be at the writing center: Deb? Fred? (Records their names, nodding at their hands.) Brad, how is the puppet show progressing? Will you be writing down the dialogue?

CAL: Yeah. Walt always wants more magic stunts but Vi makes too many jokes.

TEACHER: All right, I'll come by to give you a hand after I finish with the rods group. Alice, will you be with them today?

ALICE: (nods) I want to use those papier-maché puppets we made but I would rather tape record my part.

TEACHER: That's an interesting idea. (She knows that Alice has difficulty writing.) Could you also record some sound effects or background music for the puppets? Look, let's have an individual conference at 10:00 and talk more. And bring your current book notes.

ALICE: (beaming) Wow! O.K. I'll go with the group for now.

TEACHER: After I see Alice, I'll be due for some individual conferences with Betty, Carl, Dick, and Ed. (The children know that individual conferences are held at the teacher's corner, a table used for such activities as reading instruction and individual planning. Usually, children watch for their turn to come. Otherwise, the child who finishes might inform the next child. Sometimes, the teacher circulates throughout the room before meeting the next child in order to help the other children remain involved in projected activity.)

Following the large-group planning session, the children obtain necessary materials. The teacher begins instruction in fractions using the rods at the table beside their storage shelf. After ten minutes she leaves the group with a series of problems to solve and record in their notebooks. In the meantime, she circulates around the room.

When she stops to see what Al is reading, Al asks if he could go to the school library for another "Danny Dunn" (Williams & Abrashkin, 1979) book that he saw there the other day. The teacher reminds him to put his name card next to the "out to the library" pocket in the location chart and adjust the handmade paper plate clock hands to indicate the time he left (see figure 2.1). In that way the teacher can quickly locate a child.

She briefly discusses the motor group's progress and suggests that they use newsprint paper in order to plan the design for the heavy oaktag chart. George needs additional garbage bags. Then the teacher sits briefly with Syl and Stan who are using "Tangrams," a seven-piece puzzle with many possible patterns, and she suggests an alternate strategy.

Moving on to the puppetry group, she repeats back what they are saying when they need to clear up a point and she helps them spell some words. Since Cal seems to be the scribe rather than a composing participant, she asks him to suggest what will happen next in the script. He suggests two possibilities and the group discusses them. They decide that the next step in the script is to hide the lost valise in the course of the plot and develop Cal's idea for a test to find the true owner.

When the teacher leaves the puppetry group to help George with some spills, she notices that Tom is finished with the easel and is washing up. She enjoys his painting with him, especially the way he has used different brush thicknesses for interesting effects. She asks if he would like to write a story to accompany his painting. He does not want to write but prefers to play chess with George.

Una, who had finished painting earlier, is now at the mystery table. Jan and Rose check their names at the easel list and are painting. Ken has wandered around the room, looked at the turtle, held the guinea pig for a few moments, and then selected a book from the library corner.

Pat begins to write the findings of her smoking survey at the creative writing center. This three-sided center contains pencils of different sizes and hardness, erasers, unlined and lined papers with varying distances between the lines, and a waste basket. There are also crayons, felt-tipped colored pens, and colored pencils. Chairs and writing space face the wall or a cardboard divider, which cuts down visual distractions. Since Dick in the library corner and Fred at the writing center seem to be finishing, the teacher suggests that they use the measuring wheel with the set of yellow cards that she prepared for them. They agree.

Then the teacher sits with Alice for an individual conference. She intersperses individual conferences with circulating and helping children finish up, regroup, and find their next activity. During each individual

Figure 2.1   Chart Indicating Destinations Outside the Classroom

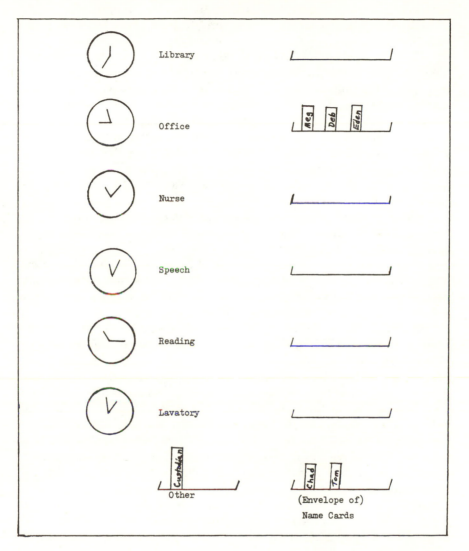

conference, she records children's progress and what she notices each one needs for additional instruction. Carl leaves his conference with a paper-back book of scrambled "word find" puzzles (Gerger, 1973). Each puzzle consists of a grid of letters in which words, listed below the grid, are embedded for the reader to find and circle.

He joins several children who are drinking from milk containers at two tables pushed together near the sink. The teacher circulates and then joins them for conversation with a cup of tea that she had prepared, using a small electric water heater. From time to time children drink some milk, clear their place, and return to an activity.

The motor group finished for the day and dispersed. Having left the motor activity, Ed and Fran are moving to survey mileage using road maps and recording their findings. They are estimating travel times using varying travel speeds. Greg is painting at the easel. Hal is sitting in the writing center and writing, sometimes copying diagrams from a book. Irene has taken some unfinished weaving from her storage box and brought it to the crafts table where she greets the puppetry group with a nod. Different children have replaced those children who had begun the morning in the library corner and creative writing center, and two boys are using Lego blocks.

Those choices that were dicussed by the whole group in the morning planning session remain options for everyone, on a space-available basis. As children finish work in the area of their beginning choice, they are expected to move to another activity. As the teacher circulates, she notices when things are winding down, and has discussed with the children their next possible activities. In a sense, as she circulates, the teacher engages in replanning mini-sessions from time to time.

At almost eleven o'clock, the teacher is having an individual conference with Dick. After another individual conference, this time with Edward, she circulates from area to area, mentioning to the children in each area that they have fifteen minutes before story time. Along the way, she appreciates perseverance and accomplishments. She asks Rose and Pat to show her the state of their smoking survey and checks back individually with the children who had been in the original rods group. She notes that Meg and Ned need more practice with fractions and that Ollie and Larry have completed the written problems. She takes a packet of additional problems from a closet and places them near the rods for future use.

At 11:35, she is seated with E. B. White's book, *Charlotte's Web*. The children are seated on the floor nearby and she reads for fifteen minutes. Then the children gather their belongings for lunch in the school's cafeteria.

Patterns of Teacher Movement.   As we look back over the morning, a clear pattern of teacher movement was evident. After the large-group planning session, the teacher alternated direct instruction with circulating around the room. She was having individual contacts with all the children at various times. This was a pattern that she had established during the first days with these children.

In this school, teacher aides helped the children at lunch and the teachers usually had lunch together. This teacher had not yet decided whether she enjoyed this aspect more than when she had worked at a private school where the teachers ate with the children and took time to meet with colleagues during the children's rest time. There had been many opportunities for direct instruction at lunch through table setting, sharing, and unstructured conversation. Sometimes she planned unstructured discussions about subjects chosen by the children in this school in an attempt to recapture that close feeling.

This afternoon, the children were scheduled for outdoor play. They could use large hollow blocks, hoops, balls, ropes, and an enormous orange and white parachute. Most of the children enjoyed the parachute games. In one game, many children held the outside edge until the parachute was filled with air, at which point several children raced across underneath it before the "holders" could shake it down. In another game, the holders all curled the edges under and sat on the inside until the air filtered out of the parachute. In still another game they shook large yarn balls across the parachute.

When they returned to the room, they gathered for a brief planning session. About half the group joined the teacher for a role-playing activity while the others read, puzzled Tangrams, wrote their findings to number problems, played Monopoly or chess, and did needlework on mesh.

The role-playing activity was based upon a large picture from the Shaftel materials. (Shaftel & Shaftel, 1967). The Shaftel materials are large illustrations of social conflicts that children and their teacher can use to interpret values-based conflicts. They discuss the picture first and then role play the alternate possibilities. In this class the teacher asked such questions as:

What do you think is happening?
Does somebody see something else?
Suppose that he felt that way, what might he say?
What else might he say?
Suppose she said that, what might he do?
What else might he do?
Why would he do that? What could he hope to accomplish?
In what other way could he solve it without lying?

The teacher was helping them to explore alternative motives and alternate modes of handling problem situations. She listened to what the children said and they began to respond to each other's comments. When the role playing began, she took one of the roles once with a child who was hesitant. She expected that they might explore this same picture a few weeks later with totally different outcomes.

Routines

When she developed the scheduling and planning possibilities with the children, this was done in a framework supported by routines that helped hold together the social fabric of the classroom. In a sense, routines can influence classroom order in subtle ways.

For example, if everybody's coats are located in a central place and everybody converges at the same moment upon that place while feeling frantically rushed, then opportunities for conflict and possibly physical violence are more likely. Instead, many teachers arrange for parts of the group to take turns getting their coats or their work to take home, thereby lessening crowding. The procedure of taking turns means that the teacher planned ahead for this routine.

Other routines involve leaving the classroom to go to the lavatory, the library, or a special setting such as speech or a reading resource room. As noted earlier, one teacher arranged for children to place their name cards next to their location as well as their departure time (refer to figure 2.1). In a large school, the twelve-year-olds' teacher has created four "passes" out of wood blocks and string with the room number printed on each block. Barring emergencies, children take turns using passes independently, limiting to four the number who may be out of the classroom at any one time.

The youngest children in school, especially at the beginning of the school year, may need to be reminded to use lavatory facilities if the facilities are located outside the classroom. For them, hand washing, which you may regard as a subsidiary function, can be a focal one, even a long-term project. This means that you need to plan for enough time.

Another element to consider when planning routines is that there are some human beings who are always slow-moving people. If you could only tune in to the Stella in a group who moves slowly, sometimes as slowly as a mistimed film, you might be able to appreciate that her turtle ways, regularly paced, will help her to arrive within a reasonable distance of the rabbit-like, erratic sprinter and stopper. Even if she does not arrive, there is little that we can do by insistence except to excite her sense of panic and ineptness.

Stella is quite different than the child who moves slowly out of a feeling of hostility, a sense of being hurried, and of not being accepted by the adult. By moving slowly, this child can protect herself from even more pressure. In the second case, the teacher needs to deal with his or her own values, standards, and pressure rather than with pacing issues alone.

In either case, the teacher needs to *plan adequate time* for routines such as washing up, dressing for gym class or outdoors, transitional activities, and cleanup. Cleanup times, emergency signals, and other routines will be detailed in chapter 3.

When children are engaged in activity that leads to real experience, when resources are seen more broadly than paper-and-pencil tasks and books, when the role of the teacher is decentralized, the underlying attitudes dictate a unique use of space. The organization of space in turn affects traffic patterns and movement within a classroom.

TRAFFIC: ORGANIZING PHYSICAL SPACE AND MATERIALS

Children's movement within the classroom is minimized when they move to an area in which materials are stored. That is, nearby materials are related to their use for activity in that area. The creative writing center, in which Pat wrote up the findings of her smoking survey, contained all the materials that could be anticipated for her use. In a similar way, measurement tools and accessories were grouped together in another area with sufficient paper and pencils to record preliminary findings. Since materials are stored in the area of use, children can easily put them back when finished.

It is simple for children to keep track of materials because they place a felt cloth underneath objects when they use multiple materials, such as baskets of arithmetic counters or construction materials. The placement of a solid colored, unpatterned felt cloth underneath objects is particularly effective for use by children who have visual discrimination problems because the cloth heightens the contrast of the objects, providing a "figure" and "ground" relationship that helps perception. This is also a useful practice for children who have coordination difficulties caused by either neurological or physical problems. In addition, a table top with an edge of quarter-round wood helps to limit spills when children are using materials such as Cuisenaire rods.

A related routine is worth mentioning at this point. Newspapers stored near "messy" materials can be used to cover table or floor surfaces in order to cut down the washing up of markings, glue, cuttings, and other residue. Implicit in these provisions is an underlying teacher acceptance that "making a mess" can be a relevant step in creating a product. Think of the children who have coordination difficulties. They may get into trouble because they knock over or spill material. When "messes" are accepted and anticipated, the emphasis is on purposeful activity and the *process* of creating. If you are a child who has gotten into trouble before, you are sometimes afraid to try an activity. But if you are in a setting where there is an area in which it is all right to make mistakes, then you may be more likely to take a risk and try new activities.

Moreover, a stimulating learning environment entices children into using specific areas independently. The teacher needs to be a legitimate merchandiser of significant activities, using the best techniques of advertising. The teacher's own enthusiasm and commitment are probably the most important elements in making the following techniques effective.

- *Contrasting a focal figure against a subsidiary background*: For example, in a reading area, you might hang up several outlandish hats when books are available that include references to hats. Similarly, a large spider made of pipe cleaners can be suspended to draw attention to a new selection of fiction and non-fiction offerings.
- *Redundancy of the product image and name*: In a writing center, there might be labels presented in a variety of typescripts and on different items such as writing booklets, shelves, and the wall. In a mathematics center, there can be models of many ways of reaching the same answer using different operations in which children can cooperate later on. Whenever mathematics is applied to surveys in the social sciences or the sciences, redundancy of the skills occurs naturally.
- *Changing the packaging of a product or service*: If children balk at selecting work with chemical compounds, you might return at another time with a suggestion for a group to work on mysterious potions. If a straightforward study of explorers falls flat, consider offering a series of "Chartered Tours Led by Marco Polo" or Lewis and Clark and so forth.

Space in which to pursue independent activities should be comfortable and inviting. Elementary school children are often comfortable on the floor, seated on a cushion or cross-legged on a rug. Some teachers have legitimized these spaces in classrooms. Even libraries have increasingly created comfortable floor spaces for reading, viewing filmstrips and film loops, and fixing puzzles.

The substantive aspects should dictate the content of area use. An arts area for visual arts, a crafts area for more "messy" construction activities, a sociodramatic area including or near a games and mathematics-science area, a literary area, a group-discussion-planning-instructional area, an individually oriented writing area, a listening center, and one or more special projects areas—each can serve a range of needs. It is amazing how many classroom settings could profit from the mere provision of an enclosed literary area and a designated mathematics area. These last two centers are probably the most universally acceptable and easily organized for that teacher who wishes to begin to decentralize instruction and centralize learning.

By their very existence, areas suggest *positive* activities in which children can engage. When you establish an area for limited purposes, it is useful to ask yourself what you would need to use if you were a child in that space. It may well be that rulers or writing materials should be available in more than one writing area. Thus, social needs, personal needs to be alone, and substantive needs dictate the placement of furnishings and materials.

Consider the message delivered when children's writing areas are in the center of the space and other interest centers at the periphery. In a sense this disembodies writing from the content areas that it should be serving. On another level, it increases children's distractability because they are out in the open. In an enclosed space, visual distraction can be cut down by facing chairs and tables against the backs of dividers such as shelves, screens, or a wall. In this sense, placing writing at the center of a classroom is antiintellectual and antihumanist.

Significant writing, rather than the marking-of-workbook-pages variety, is a personal experience that grows best when nourished by a degree of privacy and frequent opportunities to concentrate. This is in contrast to the kind of setting where everybody is expected to produce creative writing on cue. The child who is more reflective, or who needs more time to produce, can look around at other busy pencil pushers and feel inadequate, unsuccessful, and powerless to produce. If, indeed, a child is having problems with writing she may choose to stop trying or to fool around and distract others when faced with their apparent productivity compared to her own sense of failure.

Scholarship takes time that each person defines for herself in a different way. When writing is placed at the center of a classroom in the traditional mode, it suggests that content-based activity such as science is peripheral and that tool-based activity such as writing is central. When tools rather than ideas or concepts are emphasized, as is too often the case, then we have an "antiintellectual" atmosphere—although it is "academic."

An equal problem lies in the arrangement of a massive open space, with all other activity at the periphery, as in an anemically thin doughnut. Chaos ensues, and the teacher's major task becomes behavior control. Again, intellectual, human concerns suffer. The large open space invites zooming bodies, and sometimes objects, across the central area.

One teacher plaintively complained to the visitor about the children's demolition-derby mentalities. When she tried subdividing the room into patterns of "E's" by moving furniture, she found a marked diminution of roaring.

With low shelves, room dividers, or tables, you can create a variety of areas in which small groups of children or individuals can work on specific tasks. You may divide your space, for example, into "E's," a plus sign, groupings of L-shaped areas, or a septagon radiating from the center of the room. Traffic patterns need to be considered along with a water source, and a balance between areas for socialization and individual concentration. When self-correcting devices are built into activities, children do not need to seek help too often. When children work in untracked "family" teams, their family buddies can serve as helpmates.

Imagine building interest centers as spoked sections out of a centered cabinet-type core, whether round, octagonal, or hexagonal in shape. This image may further legitimize the active use of resources, equally available to all. The main concern in planning and organizing space is that the materials, equipment, and placement of activity will serve to unify the content and process, will stimulate learning, and will encourage cooperation, joint efforts, and socialization when relevant.

Undue traffic and mess are averted when activities requiring water or washup take place near the water source. In one room for eleven-year-olds in an elderly school building, the sincere teacher placed painting materials in a corner diagonally opposite the door in order to provide the painters with a quiet area. However, traffic, paint, and water marked a path to the water source that was outside the room. When the painting area was moved near the door, many problems were erased.

RESOURCES: THINGS THAT TEACH OR IMPEDE LEARNING

Use of Space

When teachers see that resources include the use of 8mm film loops, phonographs, tape recording and listening devices, models, maps, computers and typewriters where available, and interclass visitations whenever relevant, they can see a range of ways to use space.

An important consideration in planning space for activities where children need to concentrate—when writing, reading, or thinking—is to cut down on visual distractions. Looked at from this point of view, anything in a room that can create a divider, even the walls and teacher's desk, becomes a resource.

Dividers help children learn by providing an opportunity for concentration. For example, placing a shelf unit or the teacher's desk perpendicular to a wall immediately creates a subdivided space. Even two oaktag file folders or a cardboard box, standing on end, can provide the effect of a three-sided, temporary individual study carrel. Similarly, corrugated cardboard sheeting, attached to the end of a desk or table, can cut down the visual field. Occasionally, some teachers will drape sheeting or a blanket over a table in order to create a private space for concentration underneath the table. As an earned privilege for a few individuals who have proven themselves capable of highly responsible self-direction, some teachers have used the corridor outside the classroom. Occasionally, they place a table against the wall for two to four children to concentrate on their work.

As you create space divisions that can help children to learn, you keep in mind the need for a pleasant, aesthetic environment. While clutter does not serve concentration, neither does sterility. The right amount of resources needs to be available, set off as a perceivable figure against a reasonably neutral background. Where storage space has been limited, some teachers have placed curtains around the edges of a table under which items are stored. Another helpful device is to use a solid color contact paper or wallpaper in covering boxes, cylinders, coffee cans, and other containers that house the concrete materials that children need to use in constructing new concepts.

Resources need to be planned ahead of time, that is, before the children enter a classroom. Since most school buildings have been designed for whole-group instruction, and some of those that have alternate designs did not take into account the needs of children for enclosed spaces in which to focus their attention, you will need to plan resources when you plan activities. Each week, it helps to list for yourself all the activities and then the need for space, and then list the specific materials that will be required. Teachers who prepare and store the materials in the space where they will be used save a good deal of time in hustling back and forth collecting materials for the children. At the same time, movement outside the children's work space is reduced.

Personal Space. In this conception of a classroom where children are doing different things at the same time in different areas, private desk or chair ownership simply does not become an issue and teachers have moved away from "assigned" seats. However, children do need a space in which to store personal books, writing tools, and unfinished and finished projects. Some schools provide lockers or varied chests of drawers. In other settings, teachers have shelf space marked with the children's names. Still other teachers have asked each child to bring a covered plastic shirt box from home. Others have used empty five-gallon ice cream cylinders nailed together against cupboards. In one old building, each child had a large personal shopping bag hung from hooks in the coat closet. In addition, the many corners and dividers create places in which children can feel alone to concentrate.

When you find a classroom with individual desks, these can be grouped together to create larger work surfaces. A large cardboard or plywood surface can be placed over them to unify the space.

Chalkboards and Charts

When you picture a classroom in which children are not sitting in straight rows facing the teacher all at the same time, then the use of visual aids needs to be reconsidered along with decentralized space. There are different chalkboard arrangements in classrooms. Some classrooms have only one wall with chalkboards. Others have two or more walls with chalkboard surfaces. While one space is needed, whether a chalkboard or large chart paper pad, in order to record overall scheduling for the entire group, specific assignments are best placed within the space in which they will take place.

For example, while the children in a classroom may expect that they will all have some mathematics work or language arts to do each day, their assignments are found most usefully in the multiple classroom spaces where they will be working rather than on a single chalkboard. When all the assignments are on a single chalkboard, the visual demands upon many children become burdensome. Not only do they have to extract specific data from a larger mass of data, they need to be able to focus with many possible intervening physical distractions. For occasional children, transforming the vertical assignment to the horizontal paper may, in itself, prove an overwhelming hurdle.

Therefore, consider having children locate their work assignments within the space in which they will actually work. If you have an adjacent chalkboard or paper chart pad, they might serve the particular area. Some teachers use individual clipboards or folders for each child's daily work in relevant areas or for individual children who have difficulty transferring from the vertical to the horizontal plane. On the individual clipboard or in the folder a child might find either specific work to be completed, such as problems to be solved or questions for which answers need to be found, or a reference to a particular task folder or card on which such directions are given.

The numbered task cards are usually stored in sequence in a series of boxes, generally related to language arts, mathematics, science, or social studies. Task folders are generally numbered and stored in a phonograph record frame or a file cabinet of some sort. Task folders additionally lend themselves to the data bank concept whereby, particularly in work related to social studies, original documents, references, and sources are placed in the folder along with the questions that children can pursue. Joyce (1972) details classroom data bank resource possibilities that can be adapted.

For younger children, a set of tasks can be listed on chart paper near a science-mathematics center or a water table at which children pour, squirt, observe, and measure water. Three or four such charts during a one-week period have been successfully used by children. The charts would be replaced each week, with an occasional chart recycled for individual use as needed.

Displays and Educational Bulletin Boards

Sometimes a bulletin board display can serve as an educational task. For example, the recording of survey findings can be made by children from their rough notes, using stickers, yarn, or paper strips and applying them directly on a bulletin board.

An immigration map of the world or of the United States might be used, depending upon the school's population, to show where grandparents were born. Each child could represent by pins and yarn the routes taken by grandparents. Twelve-year-olds might develop a color code and legend representing the percent of children in the class, or the school, whose recent forebears came from different countries.

A related display might include a class "immigration museum" in which parents are requested to send family historical documents, antique clothing, or household goods that grandparents used. This program is most successful when the museum is an adult-monitored one-day event. The children develop labels for each family object, and the parents are invited to visit the exhibit. At the conclusion, parents can take home their family keepsakes. Some items that have come to school included marriage documents, army induction papers, citizenship papers, passports, shawls, table accessories, embroideries, photographs, a pipe, and even a braid of hair.

Graphic representations of surveys can be cooperative ventures between different classes. For example, the eight-year-olds surveyed family sizes of children in their group and displayed them in a histogram. The ten-year-olds across the hall created a parallel survey of the respective sizes of their immediate family, their parents' families, and their grandparents' families. A display in the corridor raised some interesting questions about family sizes in different generations.

When children know that their work is being prepared for display, then they independently make an extra effort to present it nicely. For example, the editing steps, such as pre-writing, drafting, editing, and revising involved in Weehawken-style writing programs (Weehawken Board of Education, 1974) can culminate in using some special paper for the displays of children's work on a bulletin board. When children's work is placed on a background frame on a bulletin board, cork strip, or wall, and several pieces are hung together, teachers should try to space them in an attractive way. Attractive labels for bulletin boards, displays, and work areas add to the positive sense of valuing children's endeavors.

Three-dimensional displays, whether placed on fabric-draped boxes or tables or hung from string or wire from the ceiling or sturdy lighting fixtures, are other forms for educational sharing of children's work. When work is displayed with care for its presentation, perhaps even lighted by a small lamp directly or indirectly, children come away with a sense that their careful work has been valued. It enhances future efforts, as it inspires them to put forth the effort. The educational value of displays is enhanced when children prepare their own labels and the text for descriptions about their findings, whether in science, mathematics, social studies, interdisciplinary problems, or book reporting.

You can anticipate display needs by preparing in advance some paper frames that will fit the varied sizes of writing, drawing, and charting paper that you find in your school. Consider that a three-dimensional display area might change location or presence from time to time. Self-checking riddles, puzzles, and mathematics problems can also be used on bulletin boards, as well as completed work or reports. In addition, the display of collections or booklets that children have put together can be placed respectively in a science center or a reading corner.

Labels on a bulletin board can connect concepts. A display or bulletin board can become educational when the presentation suggests, with labels, some ways in which children can relate the elements that are presented. For example, multicultural displays duplicate common human experiences, such as family life and careers, although they appear in varied forms. Teachers have also provided time for children to talk about the displays in classrooms and in corridors and to share these displays with other people in the school from time to time. When a child sees that the teacher appreciates her efforts by displaying them, with her permission, then the power of positive attention serves to increase that child's sense of accomplishment and success in school.

EVALUATION: THE POWER OF THE POSITIVE

Nine-year-old Hector, whose use of Spanish was much more competent than his English, was unable to do first-grade mathematics in school. However, as his teacher waited for the bus on Manhattan's busy Ninth Avenue, she was surprised to see him selling shopping bags, and regularly making change of up to five dollars. She quickly rearranged his school work so that isolated numerals were turned into monetary transactions.

When teachers sent the language arts teacher their poorest language achievers, he typed their writings (Wolsch, 1970). In typed form, the writing was poetry. However, the teachers had been looking only for discursive language and did not see the poetry in front of them. As the language arts teacher brought their poetry into focus, the children were willing to spend more time in writing.

Sometimes you can become so busy trying to teach children what they need to know in time-honored ways that you can miss what they already know. When a crystal-clear moment of recognition surfaces, as occurred with Hector's teacher and with the language arts teacher, there is a new chance to build the kind of trust that is basic to a child's willingness to communicate her feelings. Appreciating the positive strengths of children's work, while ignoring inadequacies *for the moment* can stimulate additional productivity. The finest contribution of teachers to children's expressive productions is their capacity to recognize many forms of production, however incomplete or novel, as legitimate.

While ignoring inadequacies for the moment and encouraging a child to build on his strengths, the teacher makes note of what instruction he needs to offer the child at the next instructional moment, in a positive framework. For example, the teacher can make a record of spelling, punctuation, or form needs, and then provide instruction in a separate context at another time.

The complaint of a parent that her twelve-year-old son's teacher hung up for display an abominable sample of her child's writing tells more about the parent and the teacher than it does about the child's achievements. That is, this child had a poor self-concept about himself as a writer, having been told so repeatedly by his parents.

His teacher felt it was more important for her and for him to recognize his accomplishment than to address the inadequacies of his product. At separate times, she had him scheduled to receive direct instruction in handwriting, the spelling of vowel digraphs, and punctuation.

Through focusing on positive progress, it is possible to share the excitement of seeing a six-year-old look through her notebooks in June and comment with glee, "Look how I used to write 'my.'" There is no greater sense of accomplishment than seeing your progress for yourself. Perhaps the controversy that rages around the "red pencil" correcting technique can be addressed best through parent education—and teacher education. While the adult may be focused on spelling with the "a" before the "i," the child may be focusing on protecting himself from the teacher's or parents' put-downs by producing less, less trustingly.

When a teacher circulates in a classroom, works with small groups, and has repeated individual, personal contacts with children, he is in close touch with ongoing individual progress and minimal benchmarks. He is in a good position to let children know that he appreciates their effort and their progress. Many forms of production flow from the processes of varied activities. Teachers find that they are much more in touch with children's accomplishments with this kind of continuing personalized contact. Diagnosis is not limited to a weekly impersonal paper-and-pencil test. In fact, such evaluations become less significant.

Children are often faced with teaching that is largely rote and technical, subsequently followed by claims that children are unable to learn anything else. Teaching sometimes follows those paths that lead only to a limited range of empirically measurable phenomena. Since the real world of many schools is governed by such tests, it is important to be aware of the bias reflected in any single way to evaluate learning.

It is our own bias that it makes better sense to use various ways to evaluate learning and to postpone an activity or its completion rather than undercut the children's sense of accomplishment. As described in an earlier section, when dealing with the concept of centrifugal force, the children made better progress when the subject was "revisited" several weeks after the initial discussion. Without doubt, there will always be more to learn that we do not know than that we can know. To focus on or belabor what we do not know is hurtful.

Therefore, evaluating what the child *does* know or *can* do helps the teacher plan the best time for learning new skills or content. In addition, most teachers can point to the excitement of "fleeting moments of teaching." The emergent "fleeting moments" are balanced with advance planning of materials, resources, and activities. The teacher prepares a range of materials that represents an estimated projection of children's possible options, and their skills needs and content needs, for any comfortable segment of time—a day, several days, a week, or even an hour.

The scheduling and pacing of instruction can make a difference in what children learn. When children and teachers plan schedules together and generally establish procedures and rules together, scheduling and independent pacing have a better chance for success than when they are imposed from outside. It makes sense to differentiate between the notion of planning and rule-setting in a "cooperative-together" way rather than in the sense of a teacher establishing procedures that are then "shared" with the children.

Teachers find that their management and traffic functions decrease after the first month or two of helping children consistently manage self-direction. They find that children are able to remain with a single focus for longer periods of time. They can offer children additional options that increasingly require new ideas and skills. The increasing complexity of work results from an ongoing evaluation that is largely informal and formative.

When the teacher plans each sixty- to ninety-minute activity period in advance *with* the children, the teacher can be assured that each child knows his opening activity before the teacher begins direct teaching with a small group or an individual. Thereafter, she helps them to replan periodically on an individual or small-group basis.

After a few minutes of direct instruction, there can be, depending on age, ten to thirty minutes of playing out and applying the new skill or idea with minimal or intermittent teacher monitoring. Any direct skill instruction for primary children that requires more than five or ten minutes, or for intermediate children that requires more than five to twenty minutes, is probably oversaturated with variables or is irrelevant for that time. After each brief instructional episode, the teacher circulates among the children, gauges how much longer each child can be expected to be constructively involved, and evaluates what children are doing. As mentioned earlier, when the teacher circulates, she can assess and record children's progress.

Keeping Records and Assessing

Record keeping takes many forms. Teachers have used record books consisting of pocket-size loose-leaf paper, with one or more pages for each child. They have checklists of activity plans that note which children have participated in which activities. They have recorded the opening activity of the day for each child during planning time.

After the initial six- to eight-week period of adjustment, teachers have recorded ahead of time which children will receive what sort of direct instruction on a given day. In a sense, if a child is exposed to instruction and appears to be receptive to it and competent in responses, then the teacher can see progress and plan for instruction in more complex skills and concepts.

Teachers find that regularly collecting samples of children's written work in folders over a period of weeks is not only a useful evaluative measure, but a comfortable opener for a parent conference. Sometimes, daily time schedules for each child, developed individually with the teacher, are added to the child's personal clipboard. These may be reviewed by the teacher each week or two for intermediate age children in order to plan for each child's balanced exposure to activities.

"Four-for-the-day," or any number you pick, is a helpful way to be sure to notice each child regularly. As the teacher circulates each day, he or she can plan to particularly notice "four" children on a rotating basis and record the activities and skills that they seem to need. Some teachers send one-line memoranda to the "four" parents, noting an activity in which their children had engaged (for example, "Dear Parents, John learned to use decimals successfully today. Sincerely, Paul Brand").

The main reason that teachers need to keep records is to plan activities for children. While other sources—legislative, administrative, and parental—demand record keeping, the teacher's primary purpose needs to be in serving children's development. Therefore, the following section discusses the considerations and sorts of records that relate to personalized curriculum development.

Teacher-Maintained Records.   Some teachers maintain personalized, anecdotal kinds of records for each child, flexibly using the four-for-the-day format. These, among other notes, come in handy when you need to consult with a school psychologist or curriculum specialist. Some teachers will carry a pad of three-by-five inch paper, or a stack of cards, dated and headed with the names of a number of children for whom they want to collect an anecdote that day.

In addition, the teachers record on a separate card the behavior of any other child that was particularly noticeable. The teacher notices a special moment of social risk for one child or the need for instruction in a particular number concept for another. These dated cards are placed in each child's folder, a variation on the loose-leaf book format mentioned in the introduction to this section.

A book for recording major instructional skill areas has been headed with a child's name on each page, and his accomplishments briefly noted. For example:

October 4: analyzing main idea
October 20: needs help in measuring pendulum motion
October 26: needs practice in long division review
November 5: completed book reports—Krumgold, Wilder, Lenski, Zindel. L'Engle next?
November 19: completed batteries project

With notes such as these made by a teacher of eleven-year-olds, the teacher culls ideas for planning activities set against her overall expectations of the group for the year ahead.

Child-Maintained Records. Once children can write, each child keeps a record of the books or stories he or she has read. In addition, the children's own notebooks, reviewed along with the teacher's records during the individual conference time, serve as a record of performance.

Sign-up sheets for different activities serve as another record. These can be placed in areas where particular projects will be underway, especially with limited resources. As the teacher reviews where children have signed up, he can attempt to balance their participation in varied centers.

Product Samples. Collecting and reviewing all children's work, such as paintings, book reports, or creative writing, can lend a clear sense of progression. In the absence of record keeping, such a collection and review process can also reveal a child who has avoided an area of activity.

For example, one teacher of six-year-olds saved all paintings until Christmas at which time she rolled them together with a red ribbon for each child to bring home. Moreover, the dated paintings sequentially showed children's progress and would have been demolished had they been sent home daily on the school bus. One year she noticed that a youngster who she thought was very involved and active in group projects had not painted a single time. She brought this fact to the child's attention, and he willingly went to the easel and produced a series of paintings.

Moreover, the teacher established a sign-up sheet for children to check off each time they had painted. Rather than operate a deficit curriculum, in which balance occurs largely through what the teacher notices a child has *not* chosen to do, this teacher now tries to plan regularly for significant activities for each of the children.

Formal Testing. In addition to recording children's needs for instruction and accomplishment by observing their everyday lives, teachers have been asked to test children formally. Records of test scores are used to compare schools, school districts, and materials, normatively. Sometimes the scores are used to track children into groups whose common factor is a test score range. The vagaries of profile—the variability of a child's performance on varied tasks, and the varied types of teaching styles—are less often considered. These practices merit attention for intrinsic reasons, and because teachers as professionals should be involved in making decisions about such testing.

Most of the tests given in schools try to find out how much children have achieved of specific skills, how much specific information they have acquired, and the general intelligence or capacity of children to learn in traditional modes. However, six-year-old José, one of the best readers in an inner city poverty area, attained one of the lowest scores in a set of reading achievement tests. Several factors might have contributed to his performance.

Perhaps José saw no purpose for performing on the test. Certainly, the test administrator's cool, strict manner differed from his own teacher's encouraging attitude when he read with her. In some schools younger children or children with special learning needs meet a test administrator beforehand. Other special provisions have been made when standardized tests are planned. For example, there are children who are assigned to resource rooms that have on their Individual Education Programs (discussed in detail in chapter 6) a provision for test modifications. Modifications involve such issues as: imposing no time limits, administering the test in a small group, administering the test orally when there is a severe visual limitation, rephrasing or repeating the directions, or dividing the test into smaller units that are administered in more than one sitting. Teachers and researchers repeatedly notice that children perform more ably when they are self-motivated than when their performance is solicited (Cazden, 1972; Chomsky, 1972; Bellack et al., 1966; Moore & Anderson, 1968).

Perhaps José could deal well within the trusted context of his own classroom but could not transfer his skills to the isolated bits upon which the test focused. Perhaps the pivotal skills that he used for reading were not even emphasized by the test. In a similar way, schools that test "new" mathematics achievements with "traditional" mathematics tests, or vice versa, might discover that their findings lack sufficient validity for making decisions about what to teach next. Indeed, figuring out what to teach next is a most useful reason to evaluate children's accomplishments.

In José's case, another concern might not be his lack of reading skill. It might be his lack of skills about how to take a test. Teachers who know that standardized tests are coming could instruct children about how to interpret test techniques. That is, they prepare the students in skills such as fully scanning the material; in being sure that the children understand terms such as "the same as" and "different from;" in how to properly mark with a slash, "X," underline, or circle; and in how to choose "all" those that apply or "only" the one that does not apply. It helps if primary children had met the test administrator in a less charged setting beforehand.

If a school district does use standardized tests, teachers should lobby for representation in order to assure that the standardized tests used do, in fact, address the purposes intended by the teaching. The testing field is vast and a study in itself, well beyond the scope of this book. School districts vary in their choice and use of tests; therefore, it would not be practical to deal with specific tests here. Moreover, student teachers frequently have the chance to observe or assist in testing, and teachers usually receive orientation within the school district and by reading the specific test manual and the test instructions.

Many of a teacher's most cherished values about humane behavior and qualitative thought processes are long-term objectives. There is usually a time lag between exposure to experiences and their manifest products. Effective experienced teachers have long-term objectives and they expect that it will take a long time until those objectives will be met. Different children will acquire and be able to use these learnings at different rates.

Therefore, as teachers plan activities for children, the records of standardized testing may be a part, but surely only a part, of helping to make curricular decisions. It would be equally limiting if the core of instruction responded only to that which was testable in standardized forms. Instruction should also include experiences that cannot be formally tested in standardized ways.

Increasingly, teachers are creating their own formative tests. They are giving children problems to solve, and asking them questions that show the children's knowledge by calling upon their ability to use it. For example, instead of asking, "What were the causes of the American Revolution?" an applied question would be, "How was the American Revolution like a volcano?" (Gordon & Poze, 1972). The use of synectics, a way to use analogy and connection making in teaching and evaluation, employs such questions, and will be discussed in greater detail in chapter 3. For the moment, it is relevant to note that formative testing tends to provide opportunities for children to come up with more than only one way to answer a question. After all, the important thing is for children to be able to use what they have learned and to feel successful enough to try new things.

Records and Values.   What you value will tend to direct your teaching decisions. If you value independence, then you will see success when anecdotal records show that children increasingly rely on their materials and each other rather than solely the teacher. If you value children's independent thought and increased communicating skills, then listening to tape recorded discussions can give you feedback. If you value children's original and creative productions, then the collected samples of their written and constructed work, and videotapes of their movement activities, when available, can apply. Photographs can be another way to record children's original constructed work. If you value the expression of opinions and feelings, then children could record their reactions to happenings in their lives in a personal notebook.

Clearly, a teacher's values are critical in instruction and evaluation. However, the context of a school can sometimes interfere with your values. For example, you may value long blocks of time in which children can pace their work comfortably. However, the school day may be chopped up by sessions with special area teachers and other pull-out programs. Or, you may prefer to use many fine quality creative arts materials but lack of resources may limit you to using many more re-cycled materials than you might prefer.

Records that you share with others, such as colleagues, the teacher next year, or parents, take other forms. Some school districts send two letters to each parent, twice a year. One letter is the same for all the parents and states general activities in which most of the class has en-gaged. The other letter specifies the individual progress of one child and is sent to his or her parents. Copies of these are placed in the child's docket and retained for the teacher to use the following year. Having both records gives the next teacher much more information than would a checklist or number grade system. When there is a record that goes to the teacher next year in particular, it is useful to mention those personal approaches and appeals to a specific child that are positive ways to help him or her to be productive and to feel successful.

SUCCESS: HOW TO BUILD THIS SENSE

For each of us, there are certain trigger statements and situations that give us a sense of success, that tell us that we have been productive, that make us feel impelled to work at something because we feel that it is valuable and worthwhile. Think about what makes you feel better. Per-haps you can extend those "trigger" statements to the children in your class.

Educators have sometimes missed the significance of the child's need to feel effective or competent but have emphasized the product: measur-able achievement. For example, we might hypothesize that the first grader's enthusiastic involvement with the farina-like, "See! See! Oh! Oh!" may be less likely to stem from the material's inherent aesthetic quality than from the repeated feelings of competence, environmental mastery, and prestigious achievement that the recognition of these words afford him!

Self-concept, how you view yourself, is self-knowledge. It is knowledge that is open to influence by others. As your own self-knowledge grows and your self-concept becomes more strongly verified, you become less dependent upon others for information about yourself. You have confidence that you know yourself. Whether or not your view is accurate, you will act as if it is true. Moreover, while a child may look self-confident, he may feel quite different or much more vulnerable than his facade would suggest. At best, teachers can deal in educated guesses. With more observation and interaction, you become more able to see where a child does not excel or perhaps where he does. Therefore, taking the time to build up the children's sense of success is time that is spent better than focusing on deficits. If certain experiences help your own self-esteem then you might imagine that children may be having similar feelings.

For example, where standardized test results or formative test results are shared with children (and parents), it is useful to let the children know that you appreciate what they have achieved and how they have extended their skills and knowledge, perhaps pointing out what comes next, to what positive next step they can look forward. It is helpful to tie such feedback to the child herself, avoiding comparisons with other children.

Competition.   Comparisons with others and competitive situations can serve to draw out children's negativity. A child who is afraid to risk losing may choose not to participate in the first place. In competitive games, for example, there is only one winner and many losers. And how must the sole winner feel, surrounded by so many on the other side of success? The Soviet system tries to reduce this impact by developing competitions between groups (Bronfenbrenner, 1970). The entire group loses or wins, and all the group's members are responsible to one another for working hard. However, the group pressure placed upon the less competent or less responsible child appears to be much more severe than most teachers would deliver.

Regardless how much you minimize competitive activity, the reality is that competition will develop among children in games and other school activities. The way in which you treat competition and "winning" is an important issue. Winners do not need prizes or additional accolades. They have already "won." Refocus attention on the next activity and the "cooperative" attitudes and efforts of participants. Provide children who fear competition with an alternative activity or an opportunity to watch a game if they prefer.

When children engage in games and rule building together, they grow in independence and increase their abilities to see the points of view of others (Piaget et al., 1965). The cooperative feeling of a situation where the individual's problems become the group's problems can be a positive force for cooperative work. The teacher is an important model of cooperation when he or she exhibits feelings of acceptance where needed and *expects responsible behavior where it is possible.*

However, cooperative behavior cannot be legislated. It grows first from "having" before "sharing." Children need to have a sense of acceptance and accomplishment, a sense of competence. Psychologist Rollo May (1972) contends that "powerlessness corrupts," and that "the goal for human development is to learn to use . . . different kinds of power in ways adequate to the given situation" (pp. 114, 113).

One of the finest ways in which children feel powerful is when they can see their own progress, when they have worked at a task and felt that it was accomplished, even recognized. Just as parents find the struggle to plan and limit television watching worthwhile, teachers find that, when they have taken the time and effort to insist on consistent classroom management routines and productive educational projects, children make gains in using their personal resources. Above all, the most important element is for children to have stimulating things to do in school.

Children can feel powerful through a sense of independence. Independence is strengthened when children can participate in making their own choices among those tasks of which they are capable, and when they can be responsible for completing tasks commensurate with their ability. From time to time, a teacher has been heard to say, "I give him work that I know he can do. He's bright. He ought to be able to do it." Yet, in fact, the child falls short of the teacher's expectations. Beyond a surface view, this teacher needs to look at what the child has actually been able to do rather than what he ought to be able to do. It helps if the teacher holds a reasonable, not a perfectionistic, standard for children. But it is essential that the standard of work for each child is developed and shared with him. The old adage, "A job worth doing is worth doing well," is a positive help because when we expect children to be capable, when they see that we expect that they can be responsible and meet challenges, then they have positive support for their efforts: "If my teacher expects that I am able to do this, then I can do more than I used to do." In turn, the teacher's statement by word or deed has an influence: "That was difficult but you could do it."

Examples of other statements reflecting teacher attitudes that build up children's sense of accomplishment, independence, and responsibility are:

I like the way David is listening.
There are several children ready for the story.
You are trying some new ways.

That's difficult to do and you are figuring it out.

You are really ready for the next one. You understood the last one.

I can see that you're thinking about what you're doing. That's important. Keep it up.

You've really grown a lot this year.

You are getting to be a better listener.

Do you see how your writing has improved!?

That's really coming along. With a little more work tomorrow, you'll be well along the way.

You're doing that in your very own way.

Keep in mind that there will always be more to learn that we do not know than that we can know or do know.

SUMMARY

This chapter discussed provisions you can make to build up children's independence and responsibility. We value seeing that children are active in planning, active in learning, active in pacing themselves, and active in keeping records of their own work. As guidelines for the creation of this active learning environment, issues relating to the development of classroom routines, the organization of space, and alternative uses of materials were discussed.

We also point to the teacher as being particularly active ahead of time in thinking about and providing for space and resources that create an environment where (1) small-group instruction, (2) opportunities for extended concentration, and (3) independent access to materials are natural. In this environment, both children and teacher can feel comfortable in trying out new ideas and materials because *effort is valued*. At the same time that the teacher models appreciation for children's efforts and authentic interests, each child's accomplishments are valued in relation to that child's personal progress.

From this point of view, the main reason and justification for record keeping and evaluation is to be able to plan next steps for relevant instruction. Relevant instruction, therefore, is not narrowly defined as that which can be formally tested in standardized ways. Rather, instruction would include experiences that cannot be formally tested but which you, as the teacher, perceive as being worthwhile and important for the children's growth as feeling, socially responsible human beings.

Since standardized tests do exist, several considerations are useful in order to make the test experience more comfortable for the people involved, and the results more informational for instruction:

Are teachers represented in test selection?
Do tests measure the skills that have been taught?
Do children have the mechanical skills necessary to engage in the test
     activity?
Do the children see a purpose in the test?
Does the test administrator have an encouraging attitude?

The issue of children becoming more responsible and independent
means that the teacher needs to see that there are increased opportunities
for children to become more influential in making decisions that have
real impact on their daily activities. This means that rather than merely
seeking their agreement, the teacher sincerely plans for children to cooperate in planning activities, schedules, procedures, and rules. In turn,
children come to trust the authenticity of this participation because the
teacher has succeeded in building on children's positive personal progress.

CONCLUSIONS AND REFLECTIONS

In the exemplary classrooms that were described, there was no need
for a "front" of the room when varied spaces served limited functions. In
a classroom for independent and responsible children, there is a group
area for direct instruction by the teacher but the teacher would also be
teaching in such spaces as those designed for mathematics, science, or
crafts activities. You would expect to see children talking together and
moving about purposefully from time to time. These are desirable realities. They are a natural fit with child development.

You cannot take for granted that your work will usually be smooth
unless you apply some careful thought to the use of space. Providing a
distance between active and sedentary areas is important. There needs to
be distance between wet and dry spaces. The space where individual
concentration is to take place needs to be separated from more social
areas or from visual distractions. These principles help children to sustain
their attention.

Attention is also preserved when you consciously plan to alternate
active and sedentary work. The change in activity level itself is an
attention-getting device that teachers have used effectively. The problem
of saturation by any single experience may be minimized when you plan
for active and sedentary cycles. Consider the need for children to recover
from an intense experience before they receive similar stimulation. For
example, each of us has personal evidence of a "refractory" phenomenon

when we drink orange juice after eating a sweet cookie or when we perceive colors differently depending on their background. Teachers learn to give children's senses and perceptual processes time to absorb, recover, and become susceptible to new stimuli.

Consider also that, as a teacher, each of us needs to feel that we are making a difference, that children are learning and feeling good about their accomplishments. However, just because children do not manifest glorious results at the end of one exposure may not mean that the approach is at fault. Repeated, separated exposures over a period of weeks may be needed. Initially, such long-range activity may take only a few minutes during each episode. The important sense of success that children have is an important factor in deciding how long a particular activity or a series of activities would need to continue. It makes better sense to postpone an activity or its completion than to belabor or undercut a child's sense of accomplishment. In this way, a diagnostic, process-oriented attitude rather than an evaluative, product-oriented attitude can suggest the pacing and duration of activities.

We also need to consider where equal treatment of children comes into the picture. The same treatment of different children may be seen as rigid rather than equal, because the children are different. They need different kinds of help to complete activities. You make this kind of decision in the context of each child.

Even in many special education classes, there is a preponderance of whole-group teaching practiced. Be aware, however, that the development of independence and responsibility takes time. These behaviors develop gradually as you, the teacher, focus on them as one of your teaching priorities. However, even though such effort demands concentrated time on your part, the result is a classroom environment in which you can manage a great range of varied abilities among children.

This range occurs in both special education and regular classes. Some children may need to know from the minute they walk into a class until the minute they leave exactly what they are expected to do. With a decentralized setting, and a teacher who circulates often among all the children, such help and instruction is possible.

In addition, when special education teachers survey partial or total placements for mainstreaming their children, they report that their efforts are most successful in those classrooms where more individualized and small-group activities exist as matters of course. On the other hand, the cultural surroundings and climate of a particular time, school, or movement in education—no less than in politics or the arts—may restrict a teacher's openness to seeing the work of children, or artists, or political figures, as relevant. Yet, the valuing of human beings, the ethical stance toward what Peters (1967) calls "worthwhile," that answers the questions, "What ought I do?" or "Why do this rather than that?" presses teachers to consider their own critical awareness.

As we consider what to teach and how we evaluate children's work in order to build up their sense of success, consider Gunnar Myrdal's statement: "Facts, and the handling of data, sometimes show themselves even more pervious to tendencies toward bias than does "pure thought" (1962, p. 1041). In this light, the content of what we teach and what needs to be evaluated bears a zero-based budget sort of review. In such a review, a balance needs to be found between appreciating what children can know and do with what they need to know and need to do.

QUESTIONS TO CONSIDER

1. In what ways does the physical space in your classroom encourage children to work independently? Are there places for an individual child to be alone?

2. How can you modify the arrangement of furniture and space to encourage more reflective, creative problem solving and writing activities in areas conducive to small-group use?

3. What books, materials, or other resources can you place where children can have independent access?

4. Specify for yourself the areas and opportunities where children have a choice about the content and sequences of various activities in your learning environment. If you were one of them, which choices would you regard as significant?

5. What information do you need about children in order to plan instruction? How can you collect that information from (a) systematic observation, (b) informal observation, (c) recording children's accomplishments, and (d) standardized tests?

6. Are there children reading or performing in mathematics at a grade level different from your grade? What are you doing to provide the mathematics problems, reading materials, and reading in the content areas to match their real levels of accomplishment?

7. What activities do you feel are worthwhile for many children yet which are not directly measurable?

3

Helping Each Child to Learn Actively

WORKING WITH GROUPS

Some people who work in education might suggest that teaching the same thing, sometimes in different ways, at different times to subgroups of children takes a great deal of time. However, if children can learn, can use their learning, and retain their own competent feelings, then that time is well spent. If all the children are always given a demonstration together, then some children will need varying degrees of repetition, while others—for whom the work is too difficult or too easy—will simply tune out.

It makes good sense to decide

What knowledge the children need and want in the first place
Who may need it
How to provide instruction
When they may be ready to receive it

Once this has been accomplished, work only with children individually or in a small group. At these times, two issues of concern are subgroup size and what the other children can be doing and learning with discontinuous teacher supervision. We will look at each issue in turn.

Group Size

One rule of thumb for the size of a direct-instructional grouping in the elementary school regular or special education class lies at the level of "touching." As a group sits together, the teacher needs to feel "in touch" with each of the children figuratively, personally, and even physically.

While the physical metaphor may not be essential with regular class eleven- and twelve-year-olds, the personal metaphor does operate.

For example, even if ten children need a particular skill and seem ready to receive it, that number may be too large if children need to wait while each one "takes a turn." Children may not need merely to take a turn with the activity itself. They may need to take a turn talking, or the teacher may need to be in touch with what they are thinking.

You can see this in a six-year-old group where a concrete activity with seeds is underway. The teacher and parents have provided a sufficient quantity and variety of foods such as green pepper, apple, orange, pineapple, tomato, potato, avocado, green beans, green peas, melon, onion, and cucumber for children to handle, eat, and categorize. However, when three or four children are doing most of the talking in this group of fourteen, the teacher is not sure what the others are absorbing beyond a fine sensorimotor experience.

An overly large group is particularly prevalent in those situations where teachers have established traditional reading groups for direct instruction, such as work in comprehension skills. After we observe a concrete situation in a group of seven- and eight-year-olds, we can proceed to analyze it.

10:00 A.M.

TEACHER: (calling twelve children at one time from across the entire room) I'm working with the Lions group. Sh. You stay there. (Tapping child on arm to gain attention to book. Brings child, by grasping her hand, from the door to a seat in the somewhat semicircle of chairs. Taps child on head with a pack of word cards to get attention.) Now now. The same boy. Come to your seat, away from the door. I see one group of children who are ready. I'm looking for cooperative people. I see a few who are trying very hard. . . . Mark, you forgot to whisper. . . . The two girls near the sink, hurry up! You're wasting my time. (Traffic management continues.) Everyone in the Lions group, do this (hands on shoulders, ears, knees . . .).

10:03 A.M.

I want you to concentrate. Let's look up here. Look at the words. Don't say them. Don't say them. We went someplace on the trip. Who wants to find where we went? (A child who leaves her chair in the group when the teacher calls her, walks to the chart, selects a word, points to it, looks at the teacher inquiringly, and reads the word to the group. The teacher nods and the child returns to her chair.) Will you take your turn Angela? Will you try to say all the words? Walk around quickly. . . . Sh. Over here. . . . Sh. Everyone

look but don't say it. (To group) No, I don't want any shouting. Hide
your eyes quickly. (They play a word guessing game for a few
moments, punctuated by an occasional, "Sh," when the enthusiasm
builds about hiding one's eyes and guessing the correct word. A few
asides to children.)

MARK: Is the word "family"?

TEACHER: Let's say the word in unison.

A FEW CHILDREN: Unison.

TEACHER: The word is not unison. Whose turn is it?

CHILD: Monkey?

TEACHER: The word is not monkey. It is fish. We'll play this game again
tomorrow. O.K. Quickly now, Angela, what page are we going to
check?

ANGELA: Page 31.

TEACHER: Page 31. Sh. Move over here. When I say something, listen to
me! Carol, look at me. . . . Bill, Bill! I cannot see your face. (She
reads them a sample paragraph as they read along silently from a
workbook page.) Wait, let me get my felt pen. (Walks to a corner
cupboard and back.) I see quiet workers at the green table, at the
yellow table. . . . (Addressed across the entire room. Children take
turns reading aloud around the group.) We're on page 33 and you're
not listening. . . . Mark, a boy runs . . . (pause) Bill . . . home. The
two girls near the sink, are you finished? (To a seated child) You
should have said. . . . (Children take turns reading aloud.)

TEACHER: In the pond. Sh. You should have circled "pond." (Several
interchanges, individual children reading aloud around the group.)
Who remembers the other meaning of the word "batter"? (Child
answers.) Right! (Children take turns reading aloud.) Page 35 is a
joke page. Can you wear rice? Sh. Can you wear ham? Sh! You're
shouting. Sh. Do you want to say it too? Sh. Yes, I'm looking for
people who can whisper. Can you wear belts? Can you wear ideas?
You can do this page for yourself. Now, turn to the next page. All
right, you're going to draw the picture . . . *after* you. . . . Sh. (Re-
sponds to a child.) I know. Just wait. I see two children who are not
being cooperative. Mark, Mark. Can I see you? Would you do
something quickly?

10:20 A.M.

(Addresses entire room.) Stop what you're doing, finished or not, it's
time to go to. . . .

This episode is a classic case of the management of a group that was
too large for the task that was set. Management problems undermined

quite a bit of the teacher's advance plans for children to use reading comprehension skills. The content and reading level was appropriate for the purposes of comprehension, but there were many activities, some of which were not appropriate:

1. They were to select an appropriate sentence from an experience chart about a trip that the group had taken. (This was more of a testing than a teaching task.)
2. They were to play a "What's the Missing Word?" guessing game.
3. They were to hide their eyes and hide a word card after removing it from the flannel board.
4. They were to share independent workbook work that represented the preceding day's work (page 31).
5. They were to do a new page together (page 33).
6. They were to prepare to do a new page independently (page 35).

The number of changes and the significance of the six-part plan could be questioned. There were too many different activities for one sitting. The activity was recitational, with the teacher doing most of the talking. The group of twelve children was simply too large for each child to have a chance to participate. After a child had been called, he or she tended to become uninvolved. In addition, the teacher focused a great deal on management, quiet, and order, while her own voice carried across the entire room, reaching some children whom she expected to be working independently or in dyads with concentration.

Actually, the children seemed to be uninvolved in the teacher's planned activities and were easily distracted. There was continual readjustment of seating, occasional outbreaks of pushing, and intragroup conversations about matters other then the teacher's plans. A look at the protocol reveals that *proportionately little substance was present.* However, much management was apparent. It is of course possible that an observer's presence could have made the teacher more conscious of order. However, this is a teacher noted for her hard work, solid years of experience, and careful planning.

She was working very hard to keep the children's attention by focusing on behavior rather than substance. Perhaps if she had plunged toward entering immediately into an activity, the activity would have drawn their attention. Even so, the reader of this protocol might have a sense of the teacher as somebody who was overly laden with packages, one or another of which was dropping.

In addition, she appeared very rushed. Perhaps she felt that she wanted to "cover" the six planned activities during the twenty-minute period. Consider, also, that the group size made for delays each time a child had to walk across in front of the entire group to the chart or the flannel board. In turn, the teacher exhorted them to move "quickly."

To summarize, as a teacher, you might consider that a group is too large based upon both your own feelings and your observations of children's behavior. You might *feel*

Uncertain about the progress of a particular child

The pressure of not having enough time to accomplish what is needed, assuming the plans are reasonable

Each child has not had a chance to contribute to the group

You might *observe* that

Children are more interested in each other than in the substance of the activity

Individual children seem to hesitate or to avoid talking to the group

Children are distracted, daydreaming

Children are paying attention to other matters

Some children do not keep pace with the group

At the point when you observe that the group is too large, you need to consider ways of working with fewer children at the same time. Suggestions for what to do with the rest of the children are discussed in a later section on discontinuous teacher supervision.

It is worthwhile to be cautious about using any one observation or feeling as a deciding factor. It may be that a particular child's ability has not been appropriately diagnosed for the group placement, or a particular child in combination with a particular other child do not work well, or that the group could work better if reduced by any one child. In the case of the youngest children or children who have special learning needs, it is possible that a child has yet to learn how to work cooperatively in a group.

Group Readiness

When a child is easily distracted or seems to need a great deal more attention than is possible even in a group of four children, it wastes everybody's time and energy. If a teacher insists upon her attendance then the group may become bored or the individual scapegoated. When the teacher plans individually for such a child, *ahead of time*, all parties concerned have a more comfortable, productive relationship. There is

undoubtedly a Harold or Helen in every teacher's life who needs this sort
of planning.

Harold was a five-year-old whose teacher recognized that he and the
remainder of the group of twenty-two children would suffer unless his
continual attention-getting, disruptive behavior became positively chan-
neled. Since he particularly enjoyed clay, the teacher provided clay for
him each day when the remainder of the group convened for the teacher
to read a story and lead a discussion. Everybody accepted the arrangement matter of factly because the teacher handled the situation in a
businesslike manner.

One day, the principal walked into the room at this time and saw
Harold making an intricate clay construction, joined by his own increasingly voluminous vocal accompaniment. When the principal quietly told
him that it was hard to hear the story, which he could observe from his
position, he said, "O.K., I'll turn down my radio," and adjusted his clay
knob and volume. From time to time when a *Curious George* (Rey, 1973)
story about a mischievious monkey was read, Harold would quietly join
the group. In a few months, Harold was able to be an increasingly regular
participant in large-group activities. However, from time to time, he
could read his own barometer, sometimes with the teacher's positively
stated help, and separate plans were made for him during a whole-group
meeting. Such times were when there was a more reflective, less action-
packed story or when he would need to share the teacher's attention with
the larger group in an extended discussion.

Constituting Subgroups.   Flexibility is an important principle in
planning for children to be part of subgroup instruction. The same
children will make progress at different rates, at different times, and the
range of differences widen. When the teacher provides a variety of
activities or materials, particularly in reading instruction, the children's
comparative progress may be less noticeable. Imagine knowing at the
age of six that you are forever a turtle and never a gazelle! If skills groups
are regularly reconstituted, sometimes after a few sessions or a few
weeks, then status positions can be minimized.

When a teacher notices that an individual child or a few children
seem ready to work on a particular skill, the needed instruction is simply
an additional offering in an already full program. If a child who does not
seem ready asks to engage in an activity, the child might accept that this
is another instance where she needs to take her turn. There are probably
other reasonably fresh materials with which the child could be satisfied
and with which he has a better chance of feeling successful. From the
beginning of schooling, it is useful for the teacher to emphasize that
subgroups are changing.

Homogeneous-Heterogeneous Grouping. An alternative to the "classic" oversized group discussed above might be a range of varied reading comprehension activities. These activities serve to bring together children who may have attained varied skills but share interests in common. Even for a teacher committed to books from a basal reading series, each child might select different subject matter and try to influence others to consider their "most interesting topic."

A variation of the "most interesting topic" would be for each child to read two or three books, self-selected with teacher guidance, and then convince others about why she ranked the readings in a special way. Incidentally, these are useful opportunities for children to work independently and to raise questions of one another as well as to *use* their knowledge. The teachers can find out what a child understands when the child "advertises" a book in the library center by making a tape recording, an illustration, a mysterious package marked by clues, a written statement or teasing question, or a diorama.

These many activities can take place and products can be created by children with discontinuous teacher supervision. These types of activities help children of varying attainments to communicate meaningfully with one another. The less accomplished child can see models at varied points of skill attainment rather than in a perfected state.

Interage Grouping. This arrangement is a natural "family extension" that represents ultimate heterogeneity. In one instance, a long-time teacher of a self-contained group of eleven-year-olds undertook an interage group comprising a three-year age spread. In a short time, she found it difficult to answer a visitor's question about a child's age. Whereas in the past the child might have fit into a particular "triptych" (high-medium-low) category tracking in the teacher's thinking, the child was now doing different things at different tracks of the teacher's "triple triptych" schema. The opportunities for all the children had expanded. For the first time in many years, this teacher was stimulated to expand her repertoire of activities and ideas, and began to find new resources in some of the younger teachers in the school.

To speak of the system of tracking within a single age grade within this framework is, to put it mildly, difficult to imagine. A particularly telling incident concerning homogeneous versus heterogeneous grouping left a building principal nearly in tears. She had been approached separately, on the same day, by two different groups of black parents in a small school district that had integrated recently. The population in her school was comprised of about 50 percent black children. The first group of parents, representing an earlier immigration wave of upper middle class incomes, asked the principal to arrange for homogeneous grouping.

The other group, representing a second wave of families with lower incomes, asked the principal to retain the heterogeneous grouping. The principal and faculty saw the educational advantages of heterogeneous grouping and planned for it.

Quite a different reaction came from a teacher of seven-year-olds in a large school district who said, "I prefer the slowest class on the grade because nobody expects anything of them." These kinds of stated and unstated views are an affront to research concerning teacher expectancies of children. Despite some questions about methods, research indicates that minimal expectations are indeed likely to yield limited performances (Rosenthal & Jacobson, 1968). If nothing more, expecting disinterest hardly helps us to proceed with a contagious enthusiasm. However, encouragement and successes that grow from legitimate challenge stimulate children to try expanded possibilities. The timeless work of the psychologists McClelland, Atkinson, Clark, and Lowell (1953) led to the finding that the need for achievement can be learned and manipulated. Therefore, teacher expectancies are influential in establishing ceilings for children.

Discontinuous Teacher Supervision

Threaded through the preceding section of this chapter, as well as in chapter 1, there are many references to children who are working independently with intermittent teacher supervision. There are a number of management considerations as well as curriculum planning needs that operate and bear highlighting.

Keeping in "touch" with children takes place for you during those times when you are directly teaching a small group. Keeping in touch with the rest of the group takes place *before* you begin direct instruction in order to prevent interruptions, or keep them to a minimum.

Before Direct Instruction.   Whether you are a regular classroom or a special education teacher, in order to minimize interruptions, you need to see first that all children have a positive, possible independent activity with which to begin their work. Since not everyone can be expected to be independent automatically, you may need to give some special help in advance. The special help might be as simple as giving clear instructions where needed or asking children to tell you what they perceive they will be doing. Another kind of special help may be to break down a task for some children. Still another kind of help would be to give reinforcement materials to children who spend part of their day in the resource room. See chapters 5 and 6 for additional specific activities that you might adapt from either regular or special educational settings.

For example, for eleven- and twelve-year-old children who are comfortable reading independently, it would be enough instruction if you asked them to relate several works of fiction to the author's biography. For some other children, the same activity would need several parts: (1) read three books by Laura Ingalls Wilder; (2) look up that author's name in the card catalog and select a biography about the author; (3) read about the author, trying to see what experiences in the books you read are related to the author's life; and (4) write about how the author's life helped her to write.

Planning with the whole group beforehand can serve to help them be independent actors when you are engaged in discontinuous supervision. It bears repeating that choices are most useful when they are informed choices. As discussed in chapter 1, depending upon special learning needs, some children are able to choose from among all options, some children from among some options, others from either-or options, still others from now-or-later options, and for some children you will need to direct them in a this-activity-now manner.

After you have circulated to see that everybody has begun his independent activity, you can join your direct instructional group, comfortable that the remainder of the class is working responsibly.

During Direct Instruction. As you place yourself with your group ready for instruction, locate yourself so that you can see the entire class. From time to time, use your position to scan the class in order to anticipate needs and ensure safety. This visual supervision may seem obvious on paper but somehow has a way of slipping when you are busy teaching.

Moreover, if you place yourself so that a child outside the subgroup can approach you from the side without disturbing your teaching group, another problem is eliminated. Reality suggests that individuals will need to seek you out even during the ten to fifteen minutes when you are engaged in instruction. On one occasion, we observed a teacher with a reading group of six-year-olds approached—from the side—by five different children during a one-minute period. However, the reading group continued to share their favorite passages as the teacher dispensed with each child's needs in a few seconds. While anticipation might have avoided some requests ("May I use. . . ?" or "Where is the tape?" or "Can I do the . . . now?"), some needs or requests simply cannot be anticipated. However, most of these can be dealt with easily and quickly.

Another consideration in planning direct instruction is to break down the variables in such a way that you could present a single new concept or skill in five to ten minutes. Then, the application and development of the new material takes place for the following ten to fifteen minutes with decreasing direct participation by you and increasing independence by the children.

For example, in teaching spelling patterns, one teacher presented a preprinted model of the two patterns of suffixes:

bat: batter   bump: bumper
hit: hitter   bright: brighter
run: runner   light: lighter

After discussing and identifying vowels and consonants, the teacher asked the children to see if they could find a pattern in the two sets of words. They analyzed each of the twelve words.

cvc: cvccer   cvcc: cvccer
bat: batter   bump: bumper

Then the teacher gave them additional words (sit, fight, look, fat, and so on) on cards and asked that they sort them with the first or the second set of word patterns. Then she gave them another set of cards (bitter, tighter, rubber, packer, flipper) and asked them to sort the cards and write the root words. Children paired off and helped each other.

In three separate lessons, she presented three separate sets of patterns that were taught in a similar way. One lesson dealt with the pattern of:

please: pleasing
ride: riding
locate: locating

A different lesson dealt with the pattern of:

amuse: amusement
arrange: arrangement
state: statement

Still another lesson dealt with the patterns of plurals:

berry: berries   monkey: monkeys
fly: flies   storey: storeys

After Direct Instruction. As each lesson came to a close, the teacher made sure that each child knew what he or she was going to do next when the group disbanded. While the direct instructional group dispersed, the teacher circulated among the entire classroom. She alerted the children who were scheduled for the next direct instructional group that it would begin shortly. It was important to alert the next group a bit beforehand so that they could have time to bring their independent work to a close. This advance notice denoted valuing and respect for their independent efforts. She did this as she circulated and did not call out the information across the entire room.

As she circulated, she would stop to comment, encourage, instruct, assist, answer questions, evaluate, or just to observe quietly. When she assessed that some children might be finished before she was through with the next group, she asked them to tell her what they would be doing when they were done or helped them to plan appropriately.

You may notice that the teacher always related the children to a specific activity or task. They were expected to be at work and were accountable for their work. She was in touch with their accomplishments and efforts, appreciating and encouraging wherever possible. She spent her "in touch" time by looking for positive developments, successes, and strengths. By focusing on curriculum development rather than behavior alone, she and the children could share a common focus. In this way, there are few opportunities for confrontations because different children doing different things at different times can have equivalent experiences.

START-UP AND CLOSE-DOWN ROUTINES

While we discussed some aspects of routines in the preceding section and the preceding chapter, everyday start-up and close-down routines are so important for establishing and maintaining an active learning environment that they are singled out. Every day can begin as a feeling of adventure and excitement or as the same-old-thing. Close-down can be a learning experience full of implied valuing of one another or a harrassing chore to be avoided.

Start-Up Routines

There is sufficient reason to reassess the school's preoccupation with weather if only to break out of a morning ritual in many primary grade classrooms of "Today is Monday. It is cloudy and raining. We will have indoor lunch. . . ." There is a time when educators must look at those things that are taken for granted and accepted because that is the way it has always been done, because it is the folklore of the school.

While it is important for the entire class to share opening plans and resources and sketch the day's schedule, it is nice when the planning phase can be focused on exciting content, rich possibilities, and perhaps some sense of mystery or the unexpected.

It might be nice to begin with a shared experience even before planning. Children can look forward to the adventure of varied openings to the school day, such as a discussion of values, a blindfolded tasting and sensory experience heightened by eerie electronic music around Halloween (an activity that twelve-year-olds find as engaging as do five-year-olds), a filmstrip, a discussion of the aesthetic impact of several bowls of different shapes and materials, a poem, a humor group's presentation, an infant guest for focused observation, or an oral history interview with an elderly neighbor. These are just a few alternate ways to begin a school morning or an afternoon.

One teacher who had had a problem with children arriving late placed a surprise in a particular file drawer each morning. No child wanted to be the last to know the surprise, even on the day that this teacher had forgotten to prepare and had left a piece of chewing gum quickly introduced from his own coat pocket.

Managing lateness can be minimized when there are different activities underway and the teacher can circulate in order to integrate a newcomer. To avoid the sense of "special favor" to the latecomer, some teachers have established a waiting space for the occasional latecomer until the teacher can plan more specifically. Where children have clipboards or personal folders set out the day before, they go directly to their work folder. Other teachers have established a format in which a latecomer would go directly to finish incomplete work in her personal storage area or look for her name on the class master plan for the day or continue her reading of a current book.

Beyond beginning the school day there are start-up routines that differ according to activity. For example, children learn to set out newspaper under a messy area before they begin to glue, mold, paint, or cut. They learn to use multiple materials with many small pieces on a cloth, tray, or mat. The teacher asks children what they may need that she may not have set out ahead of time. During planning time, it is useful to restate some of these start-up routines as the activity is selected. At the same time, closing-down procedures should be shared. This preparation will make for smoother transitions and less traffic.

Close-Down Routines

Close-down routines take place several times during the school day, including the end of the day and at the lunch break. Close-down routines organize transition periods from the end of an activity period to the beginning of whole-group instruction, or the end of any time block, until the transition from school to home.

Consider looking back in time into the classroom of ten-year-olds who are engrossed in many interesting options. Their teacher tried to gain everybody's attention all at once in order to give notice that they needed to finish what they were doing and then pack up ten minutes later. It took four minutes of tense exhortation for the teacher to get the attention of the children for the ten-second announcement. The scenario was repeated five minutes later when the teacher announced that it was time for children to replace materials. The child who simply had to replace a book and a pencil received the same notice as the child steeped in papier-mâché!

This tense setting underscores a useful principle: Avoid interrupting the entire group except in an emergency. An alternative procedure has improved the transition in this tense setting. Instead of telling the whole class to clean up at once, the teacher begins with that group that has the biggest job, and asks them to finish up in ten minutes and replace materials. She repeats this procedure in each of the activity areas, ending with the children who may only need to finish reading a page in a book.

In this way, children are spending less time idly waiting for their associates to finish a task. During this procedure, the teacher can see what children have accomplished, note what they may need to complete during the next activity period, or note who will need more direct instruction. In addition, this is a time to appreciate and enjoy children's accomplishments in an informal way. This teacher of ten-year-olds began by respecting the children's need for time in which to find a stopping place while they wound down from their activity. She did not abruptly tell them to clean up without preparing them. However, she did improve her own pacing so that, as in cooking, the baked potatoes were set to cook well before the asparagus.

Emergencies: How to Manage

A teacher and her class of thirty six-year-olds were in a public park with several parents on a hot June day. When the group finished a singing and movement activity that ended in each child "freezing" into an interesting statue shape, they were spread out in a wooded area. As the movement ended, one child lost his balance, skinning his knee. The teacher comforted him and washed the scratched surface from a nearby water fountain.

The remainder of the group was milling around while the teacher was occupied. Some children sat down at some distance from the teacher. Some children had their backs to the teacher. The teacher raised both her hands at the same time, in a kind of "halt" position and made eye contact with children in turn. Even children with their backs to the teacher raised both their hands as they saw other children raising both their hands, and turned to see where the teacher was located. As children saw the teacher, they moved toward her with both hands raised. Within seconds, everybody was ready to hear that it was time to head toward the bus.

During the first hour of the first day of school, this teacher had shared this emergency signal, and practiced it, with all the children. She had learned that if an emergency signal is understood and used only for an emergency, it receives immediate attention. She also noticed that it was most effective when she began to use the signal in the vicinity of the most involved or noisiest area whenever possible. That way, there is an immediate drop in sound level or activity level, which draws the attention of others.

These procedures work well with such signals as both hands up in the halt position, with everybody doing it, and looking toward the teacher when they see others doing it. Light switch dimmers, bells, and pianos are not usually available at outdoor occasions, and are therefore less useful signals.

While there are immediate needs for cooperation during an emergency, some of the group's behavior needs to be developed in anticipation of such occasions. Basically, many emergencies require immediate teacher attention to a situation that does not involve the entire group. There may be a child who forgot to take his medication and has an acute medical crisis such as a seizure or an asthmatic attack. Children have bloody noses. Accidents do occur that need some first aid. Paint and water spill, sometimes on clothing. Eyes get poked occasionally. Violence takes place on rare occasions. When the teacher is occupied with immediate aid, the other children need to know where to go for help, and how to maintain reasonable order. Children who have practiced independence and have taken responsibilities with a gradient of decreasing teacher supervision are more able to deal with the teacher's temporary unavailability.

At the beginning of the school year, some teachers have discussed with children what they can do when waiting periods take place or when they have unexpected time available. These possible things-to-do were listed on a chart that was hung near the classroom clock. The chart was revised from time to time during the school year. Among the activities listed for one group of ten-year-olds were the following:

Read a book, magazine, or newspaper.

Check your personal box for unfinished work.

Use earphones at the listening center.

Pull something out of the mystery grab bag (jokes to read, unfinished brief cliff-hanger stories, jingles to complete, and paper-and-pencil task enrichment games).

The fire drill is a regular time during each child's school experience when the teacher needs an immediate orderly response from the children. On the first day of school, most teachers prepare their children for the classroom procedure. For very young children, some teachers ask the children to walk so quietly that they could not be heard and to listen carefully for when the teacher whispers a message.

One teacher of five-year-olds shared with his children that he enjoyed hearing their conversations. However, he shared with them the understanding that few other adults enjoyed this sound. They nodded knowingly. Therefore, he suggested that when the classroom door was opened by an adult, children should continue their activity quietly and alert their peers to the open door. Their "conspiracy" was quite effective.

Still another need for an immediate response takes place if children may get hurt or are fighting. At such rare moments, the teacher's primary purpose is to prevent injury by restraint, occasionally with the help of another adult. It is helpful to step into the corridor or a special place in the classroom in order to discuss the situation privately with the children who participated. The resolution of some situations might require some "time-out" time in a place designated for such use by the school. Details of the shared-in-advance procedures and format will be discussed in chapter 6.

MIXED BLESSINGS: PULL-OUT PROGRAMS

At various times during the school day one or more children may leave their classroom group to receive special instruction in individual or small-group programs. These "pull-out" programs include resource room help; speech, reading, and sometimes mathematics remediation; gifted and talented enrichment; and English as a second language. Sometimes the whole class received instruction by another teacher in physical education, art, music, and/or science. Classroom teachers sometimes feel that the schedules of such pull-out programs fragment the time available to

them for teaching. Listen to several teachers complaining in the teachers'
lounge.

A: I never have enough time to teach. Every time I get going, along
   comes a special to take out a few children. Then they come back,
   distract the class, and miss out.

B: Yes. I know just what you mean. I never have enough time alone with
   the whole group. Between the bilingual program, the talented and
   gifted, the speech teacher, the reading teacher, the social worker,
   and the psychologist taking children out, and then the gym, art, and
   music teachers taking the whole class and breaking up the day, I'm
   always looking behind me and being pulled along. Everything just
   feels out of control! Why bother!

C: Wait a minute. What about your schedule? I mean, you know what
   time the specials come. I don't see the problem. Just work around
   them.

B: That's more easily said than done. Al just barges in and takes his kids,
   whether I've finished with them or not.

A: You know, he used to come early for my kids and would let them go
   early. They would come crashing back into the room and set my
   teeth on edge.

C: He used to grab my kids with that great tooth-and-dimple smile and
   deep voice, charming all the way, but I realized that it disturbed the
   rest of the group. So, I had a quiet talk with him. I told him that he
   would find my children outside the door at precisely 11:05 every
   Tuesday and Thursday, and that I would not release them earlier
   because they needed the time and we all needed the schedule. It was
   hard at first, but we all adjusted.

D: I found that when my children finished with Al, they came back
   pretty high also. The whole class discussed how they could reenter
   the room unobtrusively. We also developed a chart of "activities
   while you wait" just in case.

C: Before my children leave, I tell them what I expect them to go to
   when they return. Usually, it's easier when there are different work
   groups in the learning centers. When I have a whole class activity
   planned, they know that they have to come in as if they're walking
   on eggshells. In turn, all the other kids know that they are expected
   to ignore them.

A: You know, except for the talented and gifted program, most of the
   children who go out for specials seem to be having lots of other
   problems. Frankly, sometimes, it's a relief to be rid of them for the

forty minutes. Come to think of it, dear old Mike may be gifted but it's good to get a break from his nit-picking questions and teasing.

D: When the tough problem children are gone, I can plan some more complicated stuff with some of the others. I'd never want to use the bunsen burner with Carey beyond my reach.

B: I see what you mean. When my gifted children go out, it gives some of the other children more opportunity to talk up in a group.

C: When I have fewer children in the group, I use the time for a lot of individual help with skills. Most of my writing programs take place during the pull-out programs. There's more opportunity to get around to editing the kids' work and talk about what they meant to communicate.

As the teachers shared problems and possible solutions, they began to compare their schedules: "If only I had a longer block of time in the afternoon. . . ." When somebody else preferred a longer uninterrupted morning time, they spoke to the principal together. She was able to work out the revised schedules by juggling schedules with several support service staff members.

While such rearrangements do not always seem possible, it is certainly worthwhile to review your schedule in terms of how it can influence your best teaching intentions. When you have a set schedule, look for ways to use the smaller class size as a teaching opportunity and save those activities that are most valuable to the entire group for another time.

MATCHING MODELS AND METHODS

There are alternative methods or models that you can use in order to help children learn different concepts. It makes sense to use the method or approach that best reflects (1) your children's level of development and (2) what you plan to teach. When you analyze the task, you have a better chance to try to match the children and the content.

The figure-and-ground relationship between already learned and yet-to-be-learned material is central because you are continually changing perceptions when you learn. In turn, the inductive model will be defined in the figure-and-ground context. Another model that will be considered will be connection making through the synectics model.

These two models are among the most fluid models. They cut across disciplines and ages of learners. They can be applied and adapted much more widely than is now the practice in schools. Most important for our purposes, they encourage active participation by learners and increased learner autonomy.

In addition to these models, when you choose materials and other resources that will be in your classroom, you reveal how you want children to function. Children use different materials more and less actively, creatively, or independently.

Figure and Ground: Induction

Learning takes place when we can perceive a new "figure" emerging out of a known "ground." We can perceive more easily if two conditions are present (1) a clear contrast between the figure and ground, and (2) movement or change between the figure and ground.

An example of a clear contrast would be a dark color against a lighter color. When comparing unseen lengths of Cuisenaire rods with your hands, it helps to begin with a greater contrast of the smallest white rod and the largest orange rod rather than with two rods that are close in size.

An example of movement or change between the figure and ground would be the creation of contrasting patterns. When teaching the value of the silent "e" at the ends of words *inductively*, the following contrasting pattern highlights the transformation from ground to figure:

Ground		*Figure*
fat	:	fate
mat	:	mate
hat	:	hate
rat	:	rate

When you can assume that children understand the one-to-one correspondence of the consonant-vowel-consonant pattern, this can become the ground. The silent "e" words become the new figure. You create a contrasting pattern by modeling briskly fat:fate, mat:mate, and so on. It makes sense to play out the idea with card games such as "concentration" or board games such as *adapted* "Candyland" or "Chutes and Ladders," substituted for markers.

It would be more difficult to perceive the contrasting pattern if the silent "e" were to be taught deductively with less opportunity to perceive the figure-ground relationship in a contrasting pattern. Thus:

bike
hate

puke
woke

is more difficult for primary age children and developmentally-delayed children to learn *deductively*, that is, learning the verbalized rule that the vowel preceding silent "e" says its name, than the more gradual inductive method of contrasting patterns where variables are controlled as in:

fat:fate
mat:mate
rat:rate
hat:hate

Chapters 5 and 6 provide case examples of ways in which tasks have been analyzed and broken down into manageable parts for children who have special learning needs and for younger children. These same methods are useful with all children at different ages and developmental levels.

Connection Making: Synectics

Synectics (Gordon, 1961; Gordon & Poze, 1972, 1973) refers to a metaphorical way of learning and knowing, consciously using analogies to help us make new connections. Effective teachers have always used analogies. To use them systematically can help to ease learning and build children's independence. Analogies can also help children to apply their learnings and to make new connections.

How is a *horse*   like a *book*?
How is a *horse*   not like a *book*?

This sentence pair helps to build some "stretch" or distance between the referent and its analogue in direct analogies. Initially, children focus on physical properties such as four legs: four corners or that "both have a front and a back." The second question, how they are not alike, elicits more functional observations such as, "A horse can move by itself but you have to move a book."

After children explore how several referents and their analogues are not alike, they become more able to compare and transform *functions* rather than only physical properties. For example, "Both the horse and the book can transport you to far away places." When a child is able to move away from physical comparisons toward functional comparisons, "stretch" is taking place.

A child who has some degree of mental retardation or learning disability, or a younger child who learns best through concrete examples, needs many activities with simple analogies. You are likely to find that these children take more time to develop stretch between a referent and an analogue, but stretch does build over time with practice and with a teacher who accepts children's contributions.

When using direct analogies, it is also helpful to try to compare a living with a nonliving thing in order to build greater stretch. For example, there is certainly more stretch between a horse and a book than between a horse and a spider.

A nice thing about using analogies is that all answers can be accepted and there can be as many answers as there are people responding. It helps children to come up with their own independent responses by "holding on" to their answers before sharing with others.

Personal analogy, "becoming" the animal or person or thing, is another way to experience a situation. A form of role playing, personal analogy is helpful in prewriting activities. Since everyone's personalizing is unique, creative connections result and each child's connections can be valid.

For a child who needs concrete activities, it is important to be sure that the analogies do not place an information load on the child. For example, analogues with zoo animals do not serve well when working with a child who has not had an opportunity to visit a zoo or to learn the characteristics of zoo animals.

As a teacher, you can use analogies as a way to evaluate children's learnings without a right-wrong connotation. For example, if you want to assess how children understood a concept, you might ask from what animals or plants the people who lived during the Industrial Revolution might have learned about the techniques of mass production. How would the animals or plants be alike? How would they be different?

Or consider, how was the American Revolution like a volcano? (Gordon & Poze, 1972, pp. 120–127). You can see the possibilities for interdisciplinary study growing naturally with this sort of connection making.

The synectics model has been developed in a variety of ways by the creator, William J. J. Gordon, codeveloper Tony Poze, and by others (Weil, Joyce, & Kluwin, 1978). Synectics qualifies as an alternative teaching model for the purposes of developing independent thinking, connection making, and active learning for children. There are uses for regular classrooms and special educational needs. An example of an application to an individualized education plan can be found in chapter 6.

Be aware that learning to use synectics or the inductive model as teaching tools requires what every tool skill needs—practice. It is worth reading about these methods with other colleagues and trying them as you use a tape recorder or videotape equipment so that you can review, revise, and refine your techniques.

Choosing Materials

Consistent with methods of teaching that help learners to be more active and creative, we need to look at materials and how they might contribute to a sense of competence and autonomy, thereby matching materials to our teaching purposes. We need to consider function as well as budget when selecting materials. The following criteria are discussed in turn: generic, flexible, self-correcting, and attraction.

Generic.   You will find that your limited funds will go farther if you purchase generic materials rather than brand names. We know what this means at the supermarket. In schools, it might mean investing in good literature rather than brightly-packaged collections. It might mean purchasing sturdy, reusable materials for science rather than loads of workbooks or kits that have been collected by others. Particularly for science education, local supermarkets, hardware stores, and lumber yards contain much, not all, of what you may need at a fraction of the cost.

Flexible.   Materials that are flexible include such things as clay, paint, twine, art supplies, writing implements, buttons, woodwork supplies, and even moldable plastic. The main criterion for flexibility is that the materials can be used in divergent ways. Different users at different times using different materials might have different or equivalent experiences.

When you think of provisioning for learning in these ways, you presuppose active engagement by children. Children are seen as writers. They are also seen as builders and artisans.

Self-Correcting.   When materials are designed to be didactic as well as potentially expressive, it helps to change the power structure if they are also self-correcting. For example, Montessori-inspired knobbed cylinders can only fit together in one way or the cylinders do not fit. Some materials come with pictures or designs that match after two halves of a problem are put together.

The Educational Teaching Aids' *Mathematics Catalog* (1984) has an entire section of "self-corrective" aids as well as self-correcting materials interspersed throughout. Various generic card games such as "Concentration" or "Pairs" or a spinner game such as "Fractions" (Milton Bradley) have built-in feedback. Children are not dependent upon an adult authority for a response. They can figure out possibilities in a less charged, more independent way.

Attraction.   A successful material for children does not necessarily need to be picture-tube perfect. Attractiveness can be in the children's idiosyncratic sense of prestige in the child culture. Such things as flashlights, pen knives, calipers, carpenters' gloves, miners' forehead lamps, electrical components, computers, and timers can have appeal because they are prestigious in the child culture. An invitation to study "chemical identification" may receive fewer subscribers than an invitation to discover "mystery powders" (Elementary Science Study, 1974). Generic materials for "powders" are recommended by Mary Budd Rowe (1978).

Basically, when you arrange for children to be actively using tools and manipulating concrete materials, they will find attractions. Your role is to juxtapose materials and display in ways that create figural possibilities out of familiar grounds.

SUMMARY

In a sense, this chapter has dealt with the equivalent of rules of the road, traffic management, traffic patterns, and courtesies in a civilized community. However, for most children the red, green, and yellow lights are internalized with consistent practice. These various techniques are intended to support your purposes in matching instruction with the learners' needs so that children can be increasingly active, creative, and independent in their own learning.

This chapter began with a discussion of group size for instruction. When a group is too large, there are many points of communication and opportunities for learning that are lost. Beyond group size alone, it is important to be flexible when forming instructional groups and to consider the readiness of individual children for a particular group.

Preplanning, in terms of analyzing teaching goals, student strengths, and task demands, is central to this flexibility. Analyzing tasks is particularly helpful when you are planning activities for several children who have differing skill levels in the same content area.

Discontinuous teacher supervision is possible when you keep in touch with children intermittently by circulating and when you have visual access all the time. When you have become acquainted with what behaviors to expect from different children, you can plan for supervision before, during, and after direct instruction. Beyond encouraging children's efforts and involvement in specific activities or tasks, the teacher uses "in touch" time for seeking out positive developments, successes, and strengths.

When you are building the foundations for active learning, routines for traffic, pacing, selecting, and cleanup can be practiced. Then, when emergencies arise, you can depend upon certain expected behavior from the observing children.

Direct instruction can also be affected by pull-out programs. Sharing ideas for routines with special subject teachers can help you organize your instruction more efficiently. You may view the pull-out program as an opportunity for doing more work with the remaining children that requires your closer-than-usual attention.

When you plan direct instruction, it can be helpful to consider alternative methods. The use of figure-and-ground relationships with controlling variables was discussed in developing an inductive model for children whose developmental level suggests that they are not ready for a deductive model. Indeed, even when older, more able learners can work deductively some of the time, they can sometimes acquire new learnings more readily when you use an inductive approach.

The synectics model is a way to make connections through systematic use of analogies. Analogies can serve in learning, creating, and problem-solving, as well as for evaluating children's use of knowledge.

Consistent with methods of teaching that encourage active learning, it makes sense to consider obtaining materials that are generic, flexible, self-correcting, and attractive.

Decisions about your role in acquiring materials, planning, grouping, supervision, and matching instructional method and child development reflect your values about teaching and learning. When you create with children a clear structure and patterns of interaction and movement inside and outside the classroom, there are more occasions when learning can occur. Quite simply, when you reduce the time spent on management, you have increased the time available for instruction and learning. Moreover, children feel secure in knowing what to expect.

CONCLUSIONS AND REFLECTIONS

Emma Dickson Sheehy once said, "There's nothing a teacher fears more than a moving child" (personal communication, 1958). We feel, rather, that there is more to be learned when a child is moving. As teachers, we have more of an opportunity to understand what the children perceive when we can see them doing things and see what they produce.

After teaching for some years, it is possible to lose sight of the reactive, sensitive strand inside each child that resonates with the interaction or lack of relationships with the teacher and other children. Presumably, you selected teaching as your work because you saw it as a field of human interaction and changing relationships rather than as an assembly line or a repetitive chore.

Looking at active, independent learners, listening to questioning attitudes, watching youngsters come up with new connections, and hearing them marvel at a new understanding hold the tangible rewards in this work. Such rewards are less apparent in large-group instruction that is guided by workbooks, textbooks, and teacher-directed activity.

However, an activity-based humanized classroom requires thoughtful planning and piecemeal building from a firm foundation. As in any foundation, each part needs to be in place and in relation to the other parts. We need to think of a balance between a teacher "touching," intouch, and discontinuously involved so that children can be active in building what they learn.

A part of each of us does feel more comfortable when we are able to predict what will happen and then feel that we can control the outcomes. Some of us may not feel comfortable with what seems to be a sense of "letting go." We do not propose any letting go in the sense of losing control of a safe learning environment.

We are suggesting a new dimension to the notion of teachers "being in control" by their *planning for* the movement, the independence, the divergent activities, and the in-depth responses of which children are capable. If we try to confine the natural energy and movement of children in an unnatural way, then we need to spend a lot of our own energy and classroom time in the impossible task of confinement. When we move with the children's flow and channel it, rather than restrain it, we accomplish much more of our learning purposes.

QUESTIONS TO CONSIDER

1. What materials in your classroom are self-correcting? Consider other materials that you could adapt in order to make them self-correcting.
2. How much of your day is spent in whole-group instruction? Small-group instruction? Individual instruction? As you review several days

of plans, note these distinctions. At which times during the day did you find behavioral difficulties?

3. During pull-out program times, what could you do to increase your contact with the individuals who remain?

4. What models of teaching do you use? When do you use induction, analogies, and deduction?

5. When do you circulate in a positive way rather than only when there are problems? As you review your schedule, consider other times when you can circulate to provide positive attention for your children.

6. How can you vary the ways in which you begin each day?

7. What are some ways that you can reduce the waiting times for children? Plan with your children for positive use of transition times, such as talking games or a grab bag.

4

Improving Children's
Social and Academic Behavior

INTRODUCTION: WAYS TO MANAGE

Three hundred ways to manage classrooms have been suggested in the literature (Weber et al., 1983). Among these, which strategies will you use in your teaching? Since as many as three hundred choices may seem overwhelming, it makes sense to categorize them and consider the relative effectiveness of different approaches.

Different authors have developed varied categories to which you may want to refer (Brophy, 1983; Charles, 1983; Duke, 1982; Weber et al., 1983). Four main areas emerge: behavior modification, communication skills, group process, and student responsibility training. Drawing upon these, we have integrated classroom management with experiential curriculum.

Behavior Modification

Extensive research has documented the effectiveness of behavior modification techniques (Craighead, Kazdin, and Mahoney, 1981; O'Leary and O'Leary, 1977). However, there have been disagreements with this body of literature and teaching research guidelines concerning how to praise and when to ignore behavior. (Brophy, 1981; Charles, 1983). Specific strategies most often used are: positive reinforcement (hierarchy of rewards), modeling (demonstrating behavior), contracting (agreements and outcomes), token economics (rewards), extinction (ignoring), time out (separation), and cues and prompts (indirect reminders).

Communication Skills

Most systems consider communication. However, Ginnott (1972) defines the need to focus on the situation rather than the personality of the child to engage in "sane" communication. He recommends stating preferred behaviors such as, "Look at your notebook," rather than "Stop being such a daydreamer," or "Why are you looking out of the window again?"

However, we believe that in a teaching context, the teacher would need to go beyond "sane" communication, to ask herself, "Why is he daydreaming? What activity or curriculum change can I make so that he will be motivated to pay attention to writing?" C. M. Charles (1983) contends that Ginnott and similar approaches (Dreikurs, Grunwald & Pepper, 1981; Kounin, 1970) fall short of a total classroom discipline system because teachers will still need the means for dealing with seriously disruptive behavior.

Group Process

The peer group can be used to change an individual child's behavior, as illustrated by work in social psychology and research on group dynamics (Kounin, 1970; Weber et al., 1983). Effective teachers use group process strategies to build cooperative behavior. They demonstrate "with-it-ness," showing the class that they are aware of what is going on at all times, as well as effective lesson management. These teachers can "overlap"—deal with more than one behavior at a time. Well-timed praise, ignoring behavior, and promptly-delivered mild reprimands are part of this descriptive system.

Student Responsibility Training

The basic assumption in student responsibility training is that as students and teachers, we *choose* the way we behave and that we have the capacity to learn to set limits for ourselves. Teachers focus on stating and helping students to identify the motivations behind various misbehaviors. Glasser (1969) and Dreikurs (1982) have contributed parallel philosophies about discipline and classroom management. Teachers need to implement these philosophies with practical ways to bring the philosophies alive through classroom curriculum management.

Other classroom management approaches are based on a combination of approaches. Canter (1976) developed an "assertive discipline" approach in which teachers' and students' rights are discussed. Positive and negative consequences only for various student behaviors are shared. Jones' (1979) Classroom Management Training Program is a similar approach that also uses limit setting and incentive systems. The presence of a strong teacher personality that relies heavily on body language is a distinctive aspect.

Experiential Curriculum

In this book, we have selected classroom and behavior management strategies that cut across these four categories. We have adapted behavior modification techniques, communication skills, group process, and student responsibility training in varying degrees. Our major criteria reflect three considerations:

What does research report as effective?
What builds on positive teacher behavior and on children's successes?
What is ethically worthwhile human behavior in teaching?

In addition to the modification of behavior in classrooms, we need to look at the context of learning, and worthwhile goals toward which we see children moving. It is not enough to have children become calm and docile. We want to work in classrooms that help children to be involved in active learning. Therefore, it is equally important to look at curriculum planning and what we can do as teachers to help children become independent learners.

The remainder of this chapter discusses how to find out what children are really doing and specific ways to help them become more self-directed.

FOCUSING ON THE REAL PROBLEM

TANYA: RESIDENT BULLY (THIRD GRADE)

Tanya, a larger-than-average third grader, has done it again. She grabbed the dictionary from Amy, leaving her spluttering with anger, and pushed Jamie out of her way as she sauntered back to her seat. That morning, two other children had entered the classroom, complaining loudly that Tanya was a bully. Ms. C. pondered the questions that had plagued her since September: What was it about Tanya that made her so difficult to handle? Why was she always causing problems?

Despite her attempts to befriend Tanya, to be supportive of her during times of crisis at home, she persisted in her unfriendly, disruptive behavior. Ms. C. had managed to cope with Tanya until now, but with Thanksgiving fast upon her, she was convinced that she needed to try a new approach.

Where to begin! It was of little help to be told by the psychologist that Tanya was an "aggressive child . . . who takes from others because she had received so little as a younger child." Ms. C. realized that Tanya was an aggressive child, but she considered that information less than helpful when it came to problem solving. One of Ms. C.'s main difficulties in developing a management plan for Tanya resulted from Ms. C. looking at Tanya's "aggressiveness" as one large category of behavior. She felt relatively powerless in the face of such a serious problem. She had not been trained as a counselor or special educator, and she had begun to feel less confident in her skills as an elementary school teacher.

Just about at the end of her patience, Ms. C. discovered an approach that looked promising. She thought about Tanya's behavior, and she asked herself which aspects of it really bothered her the most. Ms. C. figured that if she could develop a plan to change even *one* aspect of Tanya's manner of relating to the other children, she would feel better about herself and about Tanya. In making this decision, she had begun the task of defining a problem in manageable terms. She had begun to talk about a child's behavior in more concrete terms. On that day, Ms. C. decided that Tanya's pushing, shoving, and hitting the other children were her main concerns. She could live with her nasty comments and "bad attitude" if Tanya would not physically bother the other children.

EDWIN: CATALYST FOR CHAOS (SIXTH GRADE, SPECIAL CLASS)

Mr. W., an intermediate special education teacher for children who have learning problems, called Edwin to his desk for the third time that morning.

Edwin had begun the morning with his usual ten-minute debate over whether or not he needed to do the first assignment. Having finally agreed to do the work, Edwin spent several more minutes searching in his desk for a pen and paper. With a sigh of relief, Mr. W. had turned his attention to other students only to be startled by Edwin falling over his chair on his way to the pencil sharpener. Amid the chuckles from his classmates, Edwin could be heard explaining, "It's not my fault that the chair was in the way."

Mr. W. had tried everything from Mr. Nice-Guy to Simon Legree
with Edwin, but the amount of disorganized, increasingly disruptive
behavior generated by Edwin continued, interfering more and more
often with the other children's work. At times Mr. W. almost forgot that
Edwin was a "bright, inquisitive youngster, always ready with a smile
and a quick sense of humor" according to the previous year's teacher
and other members of the local Committee on the Handicapped who
had referred him to Mr. W.'s class. At twelve years of age, Edwin was immature compared to his classmates. His reading skills were approximately four years below grade level and math functioning was three
years below, despite his tested "average" potential for learning.

Mr. W., unlike Ms. C. in the third grade, had received training in special education and Edwin *was* in a special class with only eleven other
students. Yet Mr. W. had arrived at an impasse with Edwin. Reminding
and reprimanding Edwin frequently produced slight improvement for
the moment but did not result in significant changes in his academic
performance or social relations. Ignoring Edwin led to even more
chaos!

In an attempt to gain control over the situation and to maintain his
own mental health, Mr. W. sat down one day and listed the areas in
which Edwin had difficulty. (He was surprised that the list fit on a single
page!) He found it helpful to think both in terms of behaviors that
needed to be increased as well as behaviors that needed to be
decreased. His list looked like this:

Edwin needs to *increase* his ability to:

1. Raise his hand and wait for recognition.
2. Work quietly.
3. Remain on-task.
4. Accept given tasks and assignments.

Edwin needs to *decrease* his:

1. Getting out of his seat without permission.
2. Talking out or making loud noises during times when children are
   expected to be listening or working quietly.
3. Moving his arms, legs, desk, or chair in such a way that it disturbs
   other students.
4. Refusing to follow teacher directions or to perform his contract assignments.

Mr. W. clearly had taken an important first step toward helping Edwin by looking closely at "the problem" in specific, manageable terms. Like Ms. C., he wanted to begin somewhere, and to do this, he had to define Edwin's difficulties in terms of specific behaviors.

Describe the Actual Behaviors

The teachers in the preceding examples have begun the process of classroom management by looking at problem areas in terms of function, in terms of specific observable behaviors. This focus on observable behavior can provide an entry point for the teacher who confronts such complex problems as social withdrawal, aggression, or lack of motivation.

Once the teacher and child have isolated one or two aspects of the problem area, they are more likely to develop a workable system for improving behavior. Experiencing success with even one problem behavior can lead to an appreciation of both the teacher's and the child's ability to change, thereby providing a sense of hope for all concerned.

As simple as it may seem, defining problem areas in terms of specific behavior takes practice. Our everyday language contains many descriptions of behavior that are ambiguous. Hostile behavior, for example, may imply chair throwing to one teacher and impudent language to another. Many common management problems are discussed by school personnel in global, often overwhelming terms. Yet these same problems can be described in terms of what the problem actually looks like to teacher and child, parents and administrators alike.

Figure 4.1 presents a number of classroom management problems and examples of the specific behaviors that are likely to lead to these global descriptions. Alternative statements of the problem also appear. As you read the examples, remember that you can select and define behaviors in terms that are clear to you. As long as there is agreement on the terms among the people involved in the situation (teacher, student, parent, administrator) the more specific and classroom-related the definition of the problem, the more likely it is to lead to an improvement in the problem areas in a less emotionally charged process.

Focus on the Desired Behavior

As important as the description of the problem may be, it provides only part of the information that Ms. C. and Mr. W. needed in order to develop their action plans for Tanya and Edwin. These teachers had a

Figure 4.1 Typical Classroom Management Problems Defined in Terms of Observable Behaviors
           and Recommended Observation Systems

I	II
The Problem at First Glance	Typical Behaviors You Can See
A. Suzie is uncooperative and resists authority.	1. She does not follow teacher directions to begin work.
	2. She continues to play after the teacher has told the class that gym is over.
	3. She comes to school late several times a week.
B. Jason is aggressive with his classmates.	1. He grabs pencils, pens from classmates.
	2. He pushes children out of his way instead of saying "Excuse me."
	3. He trips children on their way past his desk.
	4. His hands and elbows bump into the other children when he is part of a group or on line.
C. Libby is turned off by anything related to school.	1. She giggles and talks to her friends instead of doing her work.
	2. She does not complete assignments in school or at home.
D. Jimmy is withdrawn and uncommunicative.	1. He does not participate in group discussion.
	2. When asked a question by the teacher or a classmate, he remains silent or gives a one-word answer.
	3. During lunch, and on the playground, he remains alone.
E. Mary is lazy and in a world of her own when it comes to schoolwork.	1. She seldom finishes a task without prodding from the teacher.
	2. She daydreams and looks out the window frequently.
	3. She avoids or delays work as long as possible by wandering around the room, speaking to her friends, and sharpening her pencil.

III Preferred Behaviors (What it would look like if the problem were solved.)	IV Appropriate Observation Systems (ER = Event Recording) (PP = Permanent Products) (MTS = Momentary Time Sampling)
1. She begins work within allocated time range withoet reminders from the teacher.	1. ER
2. She stops playing and lines up with her classmates when asked.	2. ER
3. She comes to school on time.	3. ER
1. He asks to borrow materials from classmates and/or teacher.	1. ER
2. He says "Excuse me" when someone is blocking his way.	2. ER
3. He keeps his feet under his desk/chair.	3. MTS
4. He stands or sits near other children without bumping them.	4. MTS
1. She begins work according to an agreed upon schedule.	1. ER
2. She works independently without giggling and talking about irrelevant topics.	2. MTS
3. She completes tasks that are assigned in school or for homework.	3. PP
1. He volunteers comments during discussions.	1. ER
2. He asks questions when appropriate.	2. ER
3. He answers questions asked by teacher or peers.	3. ER
4. He sits with/plays with other children during lunch, on the playground, and when appropriate, in the classroom.	4. MTS
1. She completes tasks with few or no reminders from the teacher.	1. PP
2. She is involved in the task at hand, looking at her books or other materials instead of out the window most of the time.	2. MTS
3. She begins tasks within the allotted time.	3. ER
4. She moves about the room for specific purposes with teacher approval.	4. ER

better idea of what they *did not* want in the classroom. Their next step was to think about the type of behavior they *did* prefer in their classroom. Ms. C. had to ask herself, What would it look like if Tanya were not a bully? How would she act if her pushing, shoving, and hitting were to disappear? Mr. W., in the list of behaviors he would like to increase in Edwin, had started to think in terms of desirable behaviors. It is important to think about what you would like to see in children since cooperative, preferred behavior may not follow automatically once the problem behaviors have stopped. Frequently we assume that a child knows what is expected of him or her without actually demonstrating or talking about it.

Children need to know what you want them to do. Ms. C., for example, frequently told Tanya to "be friendly . . . act nice to the other children." Edwin, in Mr. W.'s class, had been told to "behave like a sixth grader . . . get your act together and remember to have your materials prepared." Well-intended though they were, these comments did little to prompt the preferred behaviors. Had Ms. C. focused on preferred behavior and commented to Tanya and other students that she appreciated it when she saw students working at the science center independently, she would have been closer to describing what she wanted from Tanya.

Although Mr. W. had developed a list of behaviors he wanted to increase in Edwin, his previous comments to Edwin either emphasized the behaviors that he didn't like or were too general for Edwin to understand what he wanted him to do. If Mr. W. were to comment favorably to other children when he saw them raising their hand before calling out or gathering pens and notecards before going to the reference corner, Edwin's attention would have been drawn to examples of what he should do. The third column in figure 4.1 presents examples of preferred behaviors that reflect teachers' perceptions of what it would look like if the problem(s) were solved.

THE TEACHER AS DATA COLLECTOR

If you had asked Ms. C. how often Tanya acted like a bully, or more specifically, how often she pushed and shoved the other children, she very likely would have answered, "All the time!" Mr. W., questioned as to the number of times Edwin performed any of the behaviors he desired to see increased, would have replied, "Seldom, if ever." Both teachers' replies were based as much on their emotional reactions to their students' behavior as on their actual observations of the students. Experience in many classrooms confirms that we tend to overestimate the occurrence of bothersome behaviors and to underestimate the frequency of those occasional moments of appropriate activity.

Our feelings can get in the way. A case in point occurred when one of the authors was asked to assist an experienced sixth-grade teacher with classroom management within the first month of the school year. "It's impossible for me to teach with this disruption! I have two children with emotional problems and two with learning problems . . . and I'm going to need special help too if they don't stop!" Certainly these words led the consultant to imagine the worst.

Initial conversations with the teacher were peppered with exclamations of dismay. Mr. A., a capable, highly structured teacher, had discovered the presence in his class of several children who previously had been placed in special education. He questioned the appropriateness of their placement (especially in *his* classroom) and he sought whatever help he could find. After collecting systematic information on the percentage of students who appeared to be involved in appropriate activities for several days, the consultant was perplexed.

Four days' worth of data indicated that an average of 80 percent of the children were engaged in learning activities whenever the class was observed. Ninety percent of the teacher's comments, however, were directed to the relatively few instances of nontask-involved behavior. Clearly Mr. A. was overestimating the degree of lack-of-student involvement; yet he was interacting with the students as though they were generally off-task. Mr. A.'s emotions may well have colored his perceptions of the class's behavior. The availability of objective data about his children's behavior enabled Mr. A. to change some of his feelings toward his classroom situation.

Through an analysis of the observation data with the consultant, Mr. A. was able to separate his anger over being left out of the planning for the students who had been mainstreamed from special education from the actual behavior of his students. In turn he began to voice his appreciation of student participation (especially when this was evidenced by one of his "mainstreamed" students) and to highlight preferred behavior when it caught his eye. Disruptive behavior declined as a result, although Mr. A. occasionally relied on the techniques of time-out and fewer privileges in addition to positive recognition of desired behavior. More detailed information about observing students' task involvement appears later in this chapter, while strategies to reduce disruptive behavior are covered in chapter 5.

Look for the Positive. While this observation seems obvious, Jules Henry, an anthropologist, found what he called the "miracle of tenderness" (1973). Apparently, for some children in disorganized, angry house-holds, the pinpoints of tenderness managed to have much greater impact on their survival as "normal" within the usually negative contexts in which they lived. These findings suggest that it is very important to seek out even the most minimal of "positive" examples of children's behavior for your recognition and appreciation. Learning how to observe student behavior with some sense of objectivity in this context, even when you feel upset, angry, or frustrated is an important next step toward success-ful classroom management.

Organize Your Data Collection.   Gathering information about when, where, how often, and/or how long various behaviors occur involves you, the teacher, as a data collector. The process of collecting data varies tremendously, depending upon the behaviors being observed and the person(s) doing the observing. While you may assume (correctly) that observing children's behavior requires you to look at your students in more systematic ways than you have previously, you may be surprised at the number of approaches available. In recent years, a number of sources of observation techniques have appeared in the professional literature (Anglin, Goldman, & Anglin, 1982; Cooper, 1981; Sulzur-Azaroff & Mayer, 1977). Despite the proliferation of techniques for gathering infor-mation about children, teachers are quick to point out the limitations of many such techniques, claiming that there is not enough time and not enough help in schools.

THREE APPROACHES THAT WORK

The observation systems that teachers find most manageable and comfortable to use are those that take minimal time and effort during the school day. Ms. C. has described Tanya's problem behavior as that of pushing and shoving the other children. Once the behavior has been described in these terms, Ms. C. has something specific to observe, in this case, a behavior that has a clear-cut beginning and end.

Event Recording

For Ms. C., an observation system defined as event recording would be an appropriate choice. Using event recording, Ms. C. keeps a tally of the number of times she observes Tanya pushing or shoving another child. If the physical contact occurs very often, Ms. C. may want to limit the time interval during which she counts the behavior to an hour or to the morning or afternoon each day. In order to obtain an accurate estimate of how often the pushing/shoving occurs, Ms. C. should keep a daily count (even if she observes Tanya only during a portion of each day) for one week. The daily average provides Ms. C. and later, Tanya, with a measure of how severe the problem is in the beginning and of improvements in the behavior during the next few weeks.

Among the behaviors that Mr. W. would like to see Edwin increase is raising his hand before contributing to class discussion. This behavior also has a clear-cut beginning and end and therefore lends itself to event recording. Mr. W. can use an index card or prepare a ditto to record the number of times that Edwin raises his hand during the morning or afternoon. Figure 4.2 presents an example of a completed chart for one week.

In order to collect data about Edwin's hand-raising behavior, Mr. W. places a tally mark each time that he observes Edwin raising his hand appropriately. As Mr. W. and Edwin develop a strategy for increasing this behavior, they will have an ongoing record of this progress. Knowledge of results has been found to be an effective motivator for adults as well as children. Seeing progress made from day to day can improve children's behavior as well, by strengthening their own sense of accomplishment, a positive outlook in itself.

Figure 4.2 Event Recording Form for Observing Edwin's Hand Raising

	Name of Student:	Edwin
	Week of:	Jan. 5
	Target Behavior:	Raises hand before responding to a question or contributing to class discussion.

	Mon.	Tues.	Wed.	Thurs.	Fri.
AM			////		+++
PM	///	//		///	

Permanent Products

Mr. W. also reported that he would like to increase the number of tasks and assignments that Edwin completes without an argument. Related to this concern is Mr. W.'s desire to have Edwin remain on-task for longer periods of time. Mr. W. agreed that an increase in the number of assignments completed by Edwin likely would be accompanied by more time actually on-task. The measurement system appropriate for keeping track of Edwin's progress in this area is a count of the permanent products that Edwin completes during a specific time or subject period during the day.

In this case the completed work assignments that Edwin performs each day are permanent products. For example, Mr. W. could note the number of math problems that he had assigned Edwin and the number actually completed. By computing the daily percentage of completed tasks in math or other subject areas, Mr. W. (and later Edwin) could see at a glance Edwin's progress in finishing assignments. The record-keeping sheet for this data-collection system could be a ditto arranged as in figure 4.3.

For ease in keeping track of permanent products, you might select

Figure 4.3   Permanent Product Recording Sheet

Name of Student: Edwin   Week Beginning: Jan. 12

Subject: Math   Subject: Reading Comprehension

Days	Number of Problems Assigned	Number of Problems Completed	Percentage Completed	Days	Number of Problems Assigned	Number of Problems Completed	Percentage Completed
M	10	4	40%	M	20	8	40%
T	10	3	30%	T	20	12	60%
W	10	5	50%	W	25	10	40%
TH	10	4	40%	TH	25	10	40%
F	10	5	50%	F	20	12	60%

one or two subject areas and look at progress in these areas. The system can be expanded to other areas as the child increases the percentage of tasks completed. Naturally, the teacher's appreciation of any progress (even if the increase is from 20 percent to 30 percent) that a child makes is essential to keeping the student motivated toward continued increases.

Momentary Time Sampling

Among the behaviors that Ms. C. would like to see Tanya display in the classroom is sitting or standing near other children without fighting or pushing. In the course of the school day there are many opportunities for Tanya to sit or stand near her classmates. Clearly, Ms. C. does not have time to follow Tanya to observe all the possible opportunities for interaction. Since sitting and standing near the other children without physically interacting with them are behaviors that are more or less continuous, without clear-cut beginnings and endings, event recording is not a recommended system.

Much more appropriate is a system described as momentary time sampling. This approach allows the teacher to sample Tanya's behavior at various "moments" throughout the day and to record whether or not Tanya is displaying the target behavior at that moment. If she were engaged in the specific behavior (in this case, sitting or standing near other children without fighting or pushing), she would receive a ✓ or a + in the appropriate column. A minus (−) would indicate the undesirable behavior.

Momentary time sampling is an effective system when the observations are done fairly frequently (five to ten times) each morning and afternoon or during a particular subject area. Although this system requires her teacher to pause and look at Tanya many times during the day, Ms. C. only looks at her long enough (approximately three seconds) to determine whether or not she is engaged in the target behavior. This system is most time-efficient when you use it along with a recording sheet that requires only a ✓ or + in a box under the number of the observation. As her teacher becomes more aware of her nonfighting times, she is more able to let Tanya know that she recognizes her acceptable behavior. Figure 4.4 presents an example of a recording sheet that can be completed daily for a week at a time.

Momentary time sampling can be used for a variety of behavior categories such as "engaged in appropriate behavior," not thumbsucking or not nailbiting, and on-task behavior. A detailed discussion of on-task behavior and suggestions for observing and increasing it appear in a later section of this chapter.

Figure 4.4 Momentary Time Sampling Observation

Name of Child: Tanya

Week Beginning: November 6

Target Behavior: Nonfighting

Observations

Days	1	2	3	4	5	6	7	8	9	10	Percentage Nonfighting
M	+	−	−	−	+	+	−	+	−	+	5/10=50%
T	−	−	+	+	−	−	−	+	+	+	5/10=50%
W	+	+	−	−	−	+	+	−	−	−	4/10=40%
TH	−	−	−	+	+	+	−	+	−	−	4/10=40%
F	+	+	+	−	−	−	+	−	+	+	6/10=60%

Event recording, permanent products, and momentary time sampling are three observation approaches that teachers have found effective and comfortable for use in the classroom. The fourth column in figure 4.1 presents suggested observation systems for use in developing a number of behaviors necessary for a well-managed classroom.

ENCOURAGING DESIRABLE BEHAVIOR PATTERNS

Incentives are important for each of us—and that includes our students! In order to appreciate the role that incentives play for us, ask yourself the following questions.

1. *How long would I work at my present job (if working) if I did not receive a paycheck every week or two?* During a good period, you might respond, "two or three weeks." And the only reason that most of us would last the two or three weeks is that we enjoy what we are doing or at least we enjoy the company of our coworkers. There is ample evidence that our students also perform better when their efforts are appreciated (Aaron & Bostow, 1978; Becker, Madsen, Arnold, & Thomas, 1967; Madsen, Becker, & Thomas, 1968; Sulzur-Azaroff & Meyer, 1977; Zimmerman & Zimmerman, 1962).
2. *When I am faced with a difficult task, what gets me to start it? To finish it?* The prospect of sitting down to prepare twenty-five individual folders for your fourth-grade students may not provide the high-

point of your Saturday. If you plan to attend a concert later the same evening, however, and if you have been invited to spend Sunday with friends, you are more likely to start your work earlier and proceed with it than you would if there were not special plans scheduled for after its completion.

An additional effective reward for adults or children can be any behavior that is a preferred activity that often takes place. For example, the gregarious part of you, facing twenty-five compositions to edit might find it helpful to complete half before taking a telephone break. Similarly, the child in your classroom who frequently seeks out the hamster cage can look forward to a visit there after cleaning up a science activity.

The theory behind this approach is drawn from the work of David Premack (1965) and technically is referred to as the "Premack Principle." For many of us, anticipation of the difficulty involved in task completion effectively prevents us from actually starting the task . . . and from realizing that once begun, the task is more manageable than we had thought. One effective strategy for getting started at a task is to set a short time limit and work at the task for only that amount of time. Once the work has been started, you are likely to want to continue for a longer period of time. Of course, you may extend the time limit several times before taking a short break. The difficult job of beginning has been completed successfully.

For some of our students, becoming involved in learning activities may be as difficult as it would be for us to address Congress, write a sonnet, or center clay on a potter's wheel. A major task that we face as teachers is arranging appropriate incentives to help students start and break up their work requirements into manageable units.

3. *What type of feedback do I like to receive after completing something?* Remember the time that you struggled to bake bread? The recipe had appeared easy enough. You were determined to master kneading (even after your hands had become tired and very sticky). You were careful to follow the instructions, although you almost gave up the idea of bread baking altogether when you discovered that the total amount of time involved was three hours! After baking the loaves for the required time, you presented them to your family.

"They're so flat! I thought you were baking bread with yeast in it."

"Gee, I thought I would like it when I smelled it baking. I'm not hungry now."

"You must have made a mistake—that recipe has been working fine for me for years."

Music to your ears? Not exactly. Where is the recognition for your labors? Where is the appreciation for your good idea . . . and your three hours? It is easy to become locked into the practice of giving praise to our students for their products only (good ones at that). Yet, in the example above, what is missing is positive feedback for the attempt made, for the effort—even if the product did not turn out in the anticipated manner. There is, after all, an act of love for your family that is played out in placing three hours of your life in an effort that might please them.

Selecting Incentives

The selection of an incentive system for children in your classroom involves knowledge of students' likes and dislikes, practical factors such as time, space, and money limitation. You also need to assess your own preferences about the various options. Before moving to the details of selecting specific types of feedback and activities for your students, let us look at a framework for choosing types of incentives. The development and use of an incentive system may be criticized by well-meaning colleagues who fear that children will become dependent on external rewards and therefore unable to function without them in later years. This criticism may be accurate in some situations where a teacher arbitrarily decides that "happy face stickers" and raisins are appropriate rewards since they are "the only ones that work" and where children work for fear or love of the teacher rather than for the inner value and satisfaction of the work. Unfortunately, the selection and continued use of this type of incentive are likely to occur in other situations if there is no overall plan governing the selection and use of rewards. It becomes important to provide only the incentive that is necessary to help children feel successful and satisfied with their work.

Social Attention and Approval.   If our goal in choosing an incentive system is to pick one that can be used and maintained in the classroom with ease, we must choose incentives that are currently available in this setting. We are fortunate that appreciative comments, smiles, and gestures from teacher and peers have been found to be powerful rewards (Broden, Copeland, Beasley, & Hall, 1977; Clements & Tracy, 1977; O'Leary & O'Leary, 1977), and we know that the potential for positive contributions from teacher and peers exists in every classroom! Although we may have to rearrange the behaviors toward which we direct our attention and the means by which we give our attention, we have discovered the most natural incentive in any classroom: social attention and approval.

Self-Reinforcement.   Seriously disruptive behavior will benefit from the continuum of techniques described later in this chapter more than it would from simple teacher approval and ignoring alone. A recent review of research supports this position (Weber et al., 1983). Figure 4.5 illustrates options along this continuum.

Historically, adults have used the least natural rewards for influencing younger children and developmentally delayed individuals. Rather than assume that you have to start at the low end of the hierarchy, it makes sense to start with the most natural incentives and move along the continuum only if these do not work.

Teacher approval can be effective for those behaviors that are annoying but tolerable, such as talking at the wrong time or wandering around the room. Brophy (1981) provides guidelines for effective versus ineffective teacher praise. He recommends that the most helpful teacher comments are directed toward individuals who demonstrate specific desired behavior, such as contributing appropriately to class discussion or working at one's own table, *when* they are engaged in these behaviors. The more personalized these comments are, and the more they attribute the child's success to his own efforts, the more likely are these comments to be effective. In developing a hierarchy of incentives that is natural to the learning environment, social attention and approval from teacher and peers would be close to the top. At the top of the list would be the

Figure 4.5   A Hierarchy of Incentives

Most Natural	Self-Approval
	(e.g., for its own sake)
	Social Approval
	(e.g., teacher approval)
	Activities
	(e.g., high interest)
	Exchange System
	(e.g., points)
	Tangible Incentives
	(e.g., stickers)
Least Natural	Edible Incentives
	(e.g., raisins)

category of self-reinforcement, whereby tasks are completed solely for the feeling of accomplishment that follows it. Self-reinforcement is certainly natural and unobtrusive in a classroom. It is also seldom sufficient for most of us, teachers and students alike. When was the last time you taught for a month without pay?

Activities: Children Enjoy Responsibility.   Moving down the hierarchy from self-reinforcement and social attention we find the category of activity incentives. This category includes a wide variety of activities that occur frequently within a classroom. Allowing the child to act as messenger or paper monitor has been used traditionally by teachers as student responsibilities. Adapting these responsibilities as activity incentives requires only that a child earn the privilege of doing the errands or distributing paper *after* she or he has completed prespecified work assignments. Additional examples of activity incentives abound when you consider that any learning activity gains more status when a child must earn the privilege of participating in it. Teachers have used additional time in the science center as an incentive to complete math problems without wandering around the room or calling to one's neighbors. Reading library books, completing math puzzles, constructing a diorama, and adapting a social studies unit into a role-playing scenario are additional examples of activity incentives that occur naturally within the classroom setting.

Concrete Aids.   If social approval and activity incentives are insufficient to motivate all the children in your class, move down the hierarchy to an exchange system. Simply described, an exchange system refers to any program where check marks, stars, tokens, or points are "cashed in" or exchanged for something else (for example, listening to books on tape, writing in a diary, acting as messenger; writing a "Happygram" to parents).

The advantage of an exchange system is that it allows you to give the child(ren) more immediate and concrete indication of approval and accomplishment. Tanya, for example, may have difficulty waiting until it is time for her privilege of taking a message to the principal. If she is unable to wait for her reward, to delay gratification in a sense, she may benefit from getting a point each time she is observed by her teacher to be acting appropriately. When she has received five points, she may carry the message to the main office. Whenever the point is recorded, the teacher makes sure to voice her appreciation of Tanya's efforts. In this way, Tanya develops even more positive associations to her teacher's comments.

The goal of this, and any exchange system, is to enable a child to make the connection between appropriate behavior and positive feedback from the environment. Gradually the exchange system can be eliminated as Tanya learns that she can participate in enjoyable activities as a consequence of improved behavior. The choice of stars, check marks, points, or tokens is an important one since research demonstrates that children's preferences may differ from those of the teacher. Whenever possible, children should participate in selecting their own incentives (Bassett, Blanchard, & Koshland, 1977; Raschke, 1979, 1981).

Figure 4.5 presents a comprehensive hierarchy of incentives. The use of tangible incentives (trinkets, puzzles, toys) and edible incentives (raisins, candy, popcorn) seldom is warranted in school settings. Small toys and food have been used successfully in certain restricted settings, but they are not natural in schools.

Whenever you use incentives in addition to social attention and approval, your goal is to move down the hierarchy only as far as necessary to increase appropriate behavior. After the child makes progress, gradually move up the hierarchy until the behavior changes are maintained by social and self-approval and occasional activity incentives. The "how to" of moving up the hierarchy depends on your careful observation and willingness to accept what you see, and plan for what is reasonable. Five minutes of attention may lead more reasonably to seven minutes before the desired goal of twenty minutes.

Once you see that the child is doing regularly what you had agreed upon, you gradually give the token or reward less frequently. At the same time, you are pairing the tangible reward with social rewards, such as, teacher praise and approval. For example:

Step 1. Complete each activity

Earn one ticket (exchange system).
"You must feel good about your work: You worked hard."

Step 2. Complete two activities

Earn one ticket.
"You're finishing your work so efficiently now that you are grown up enough to finish more work."

Step 3. Complete two activities that require longer time and more effort

Earn entry to high interest activity.
"You've worked so carefully that

you can be responsible for
teaching the kindergarten children about our class snake."

Step 4.   Maintain level of task   Periodic teacher praise and entry
      completion   into high interest activity.

ON-TASK BEHAVIOR

No book on classroom management would be complete without
some discussion of on-task behavior. In fact, many of the management
difficulties that teachers talk about have to do with children *not* being
involved in whatever is the appropriate task at a given time. Just listen for
a minute outside the door of a "typical" fourth-grade classroom and you
are likely to hear the following:

"Joanne, stop that this minute! Who gave you permission to get the
ball for outdoor gym?"

"All right class, we'll wait . . . as long as you continue to talk instead
of listening to me you'll never get to finish your lesson . . . and you'll be
late for gym."

"Tommy, are you reading that comic book again? When will you
learn to follow the directions I give you!"

Responses from the Children

Having overheard these not-so-unusual teacher comments, let us
imagine what some of the children are saying to themselves in response.
It is helpful to consider the children who are the focus of teacher comments as target children. However, other children sitting near the target
students are certainly observing these events.

Consider Joanne, the target child in the teacher's first comment, and
what she might be thinking and feeling: "There he goes again! All I
wanted to do was get the ball first. Oh well, if I sit down for a minute and
just look at the book, he'll find someone else to yell at. Then I can get it."
This may not be the repentant attitude that Mr. G. was hoping for when
he told Joanne to stop what she had been doing. Nor is it likely that his
comment would have a lasting effect, given Joanne's last sentence. In
fact, Joanne was overheard still later saying to a pal, "Did you see how
mad Mr. G. got? He sure looked funny!" The net effect of Mr. G.'s
negative comment seems to have been a temporary halt in Joanne's

march to the gym ball, coupled with an enormous sense of power given to Joanne, who was able to get her teacher mad and make him look "funny."

The children who were the targets of Mr. G.'s statement about being late for gym comprised only about a third of the class. Some could be observed chatting about last night's Superhero television special. One child could be seen tracing around his fingers on the edge of his worksheet. Several other children were comparing sneakers to see whose had the most "interesting" holes and worn marks. Two other children were looking back and forth between the teacher's examples on the board and their own sentences, making faces and saying, "This isn't right . . . it doesn't look like Mr. G.'s."

Some of these target children might be saying to themselves, "Who cares if we're late. We're always late." The child who was busily tracing his fingers might think, "Good, I hate gym. Nobody picks me for their team." The sneaker connoisseurs might comment (to themselves or aloud), "Gym . . . that's right, we have gym today." One of the two youngsters who appeared to have some difficulty with her sentence compositions might be wondering, "How come he's making us miss some of gym? We didn't ask to have such hard work to do. Forget it! I can't do it right anyway. I'm not doing anymore."

It would appear that none of the children were inspired to get down to business and return to task. In fact, quite the opposite appears to have happened. Those children who were on-task (comparing their written products with the teacher's) but who were talking about the task may have decided that it was not worth the effort to work since the teacher already has scolded the whole group. The finger-tracer was happy that his delaying tactics had been so successful! And the sneaker group apparently only heard the end of the teacher's comment about gym and were glad to know that they were scheduled for it that day.

Now that we've considered the possible reactions of some of the target children in Mr. G.'s class, let us put ourselves in the position of some of the children who are "observing" the targets. Pretend that you are a child who is working hard at writing when the teacher makes his first statement: "I've been looking forward to gym all morning. At least there you can run around, throw balls and have fun. This language arts is not my favorite thing to do, but I might as well get through it as best I can so that I won't miss a minute of gym. What is he saying now? It's not fair. I'm going to have to be late anyway just because of some of the other kids. What's the use of doing all this work!"

Given this student's discouraged response to her teacher's comment, it is likely that she will think twice before organizing her own time as effectively as she had done this morning. In fact, she may decide to join those children who are not as involved in the learning activity since the outcome (missing some of the gym class) is the same for all, workers and nonworkers alike.

Describing On-Task Behavior

What is it that the teacher in our example is trying to accomplish? What exactly is on-task behavior? Definitions of on-task behavior vary from setting to setting, across different times of day and often from teacher to teacher—and that is as it should be. When a person is on-task, his attention is to, or his participation is related to, the task at hand. For example, during an indoor lunch period, playing knock-hockey or using lotto games may be equally appropriate (hence, on-task) activities. Looking at the chalkboard where students are completing problems during a math lesson, participating in a group discussion during social studies, and talking to a friend about the current assignment in a setting where the teacher encourages socialization as an important component of learning are additional examples of on-task behaviors.

By extension, any activity that is different from the one(s) selected as appropriate by the teacher is likely to be considered off-task, at least by the adult(s) in the classroom. Examples of off-task behavior come quickly to mind. (Remember our eavesdropping on the fourth-grade classroom!) They include such activities as doodling on worksheets, playing with ballpoint-pen-parts collections or three-dimensional puzzles, roaming around the room (carefully avoiding any work area along the way), or getting more drinks of water than generally are permitted.

Let us return to the fourth-grade classroom mentioned above, and to the teacher's valiant attempts to bring children back to task. Why are we educators interested in developing on-task behavior in our students? What has caused us to focus on pupil attention as an important indicator of such factors as teacher effectiveness (Morrison, 1926), pupil achievement (Lahaderne, 1968; Shannon, 1942), and students' attitudes toward school (Lahaderne, 1968)?

We observe that when children are involved in appropriate activities (whether teacher- or student-selected), they are less likely to be disruptive and to serve as a negative behavior model for other students. The ripple effect, where teacher behavior toward a target child has impact on an observing child, extends in both directions. The more children are on-task, the more likely they are to demonstrate appropriate behavior to others and to be appreciated by the teacher. In contrast, the more a child is off-task (whether the behavior is disruptive or just ineffective as far as task completion is concerned) the more likely he or she is to pull other children away from appropriate activities and, possibly, to receive negative attention from the teacher. Research conducted on effective schools points to time on-task as a more important factor in learning than resources per se (Curran, 1982).

Observing and Encouraging On-Task Behavior

Having convinced ourselves that on-task behavior is desirable in a classroom, let us look at ways in which we can encourage this in our students. As we discovered at the beginning of this chapter, there are certain steps to complete if we are to be successful change agents.

1. **Defining the problem.** Using positive statements, describe the problem to be solved. Let's assume that the teacher we overheard trying to bring the fourth graders back to task had a language arts lesson to complete before the gym period began. With some encouragement from a helpful consultant who asked, "What would the on-task behavior look like if you saw it?" he might have described his problem-to-be-solved in this manner:

> Students will listen to the instructions for their language arts worksheet without talking or wandering.
> Students will work on their language arts activity (reading the directions, writing the responses) without walking around the room or talking loudly.

2. **Collecting information.** Gather data about the behavior(s) you want to change. Based on the teacher's description of desired behavior, two methods of data collection are appropriate. Although "listening to instructions" may involve a variety of appropriate child behaviors (for example, eyes facing the teacher, eyes looking at the worksheet, eyes closed), the teacher makes a judgment about which behaviors he considers to be on-task for this listening activity. After reflecting on his own listening experiences at a concert, in a graduate school class, or during a tennis lesson, he decides that the children will be considered on-task when they are seated and they

> Look at him or the worksheet without talking to anyone
> Raise a hand for clarification
> Keep their eyes closed except when he directs them to follow a sequence of workbook instructions.

One measure of on-task behavior in this situation is the number of examples completed in the language arts lesson (permanent products). Since most of the child behaviors occur over a period of time and have no clear-cut beginning or end, momentary time sampling is the preferred way to collect data. The procedure for collecting information about on-task behavior through momentary time sampling is simple and quick, after an initial practice period:

> Several times during the lesson, look at each student for a few seconds (count 1, 2, 3).
>
> If the student appears on-task, that is, she or he is doing what ought to be done at that time, mark a + in the space next to the name. If the student is *not* doing what you consider appropriate for that time, mark a − next to the name.
>
> Continue looking at the students periodically. When you have completed five observations per child, compute the number of on-task observations divided by the total number of observations completed. Place the percent obtained in the appropriate column.

Figure 4.6 presents a sample of a recording form completed for some of the children in Mr. G.'s class. This form may be expanded to include as many children as are present in a classroom.

In order to obtain an accurate picture of on-task behavior in a classroom, the teacher would observe on-task behavior for a week before beginning any program to increase the children's task involvement. Once this initial period of information gathering is over, the teacher may begin to focus his or her attention on those children who are on-task. Frequent appreciative comments and smiles for children who are working by themselves or cooperatively in small groups should replace the previous scolding of children who are not working.

3. Developing a practical incentive system.   In the early stages of increasing task involvement, it is important to positively recognize improvement in on-task behavior rather than to withhold this recognition until a specific level of on-task behavior occurs. Initially you may find that the average percentage of on-task behavior in your class is 50 percent. Using the concept of an On-Task Club, you advise the children that membership in this club depends upon an *improvement* of at least 10 percent over their previous week's average. Once the children have begun to increase on-task behavior, you may raise the criterion for club admission to a set level of 80 percent.

Figure 4.6 Momentary Time Sampling: On-Task Observation Form
_____

Teacher's Name: Mr. G.   Date: March 1

Activity: Independent completion of language arts
            assignment.

Time Begin: 10:15   Time End: 10:25

Observations

Children's Names	1	2	3	4	5	Percentage On-task
Joanne	+	+	−	−	+	3/5=60%
Tommy	−	−	−	+	−	1/5=20%
Jenni	+	+	+	+	+	5/5=100%
Todd	+	−	−	+	+	3/5=60%
Adam	+	+	+	+	−	4/5=80%
Meg	+	+	+	+	+	5/5=100%

With the incentive hierarchy in mind, positive consequences for on-task behavior might begin with the teacher's recognition of appropriate behavior. As an additional social incentive, membership in the On-Task Club allows children to receive recognition from peers as well as the teacher. Support from the children's parents can be obtained by sending home "Happygrams" that report improved on-task behavior. These messages to the home often provide a sharp contrast to the more typical notes to parents about inappropriate behavior.

If additional incentives are necessary, activities such as listening to tapes, participating in math games, or using arts and crafts materials may be available to children after they have reached a specified level of on-task behavior for the day.

SUMMARY

Although a number of alternative approaches to classroom management were discussed, this chapter emphasized a plan based upon observing children's behavior, setting reasonable goals, and arranging incentives for their attainment in the classroom. The major steps in this plan are

1. Defining a problem in terms of specific observable behaviors.
2. Describing the positive behaviors that you want to increase.
3. Describing the negative behaviors that you want to decrease.
4. Selecting the observation system that you can manage in your classroom.
5. Developing an incentive system that works for your students.
6. Arranging logical consequences for inappropriate behavior.

Several observation systems were discussed in detail. The following systems are manageable and likely to be effective in most classroom situations:

Event recording—recording the frequency of the behavior in question

Permanent products—recording the number of completed tasks

Momentary time sampling—periodically observing whether or not a child is on-task.

When a problem comes up, many adults tend to "get tough," reprimand, and blame children. Children will work to avoid a reprimand rather than develop personal motives for changing their behavior. This builds dependence on outside authority rather than self-reliance. An unfortunate spin-off of reliance on reprimands and other punishments is increased fibbing and escape behavior.

Incentives work best when they are as natural as possible to the classroom environment and when they are valued highly by students. When selecting incentives, begin as high as possible on the hierarchy of reinforcers presented in this chapter, and move down to more concrete, tangible incentives only as you need to bring about beginning behavior change.

Teacher appreciation and approval played a prominent role in improving and changing behavior. Guidelines included giving specific information to children about what they have accomplished. Also, teachers underline the child's intrinsic ownership of, and responsibility for, her or his behavior and effort. For example, rather than say, "I am proud of you," the teacher would say, "That was hard to do but you did it."

CONCLUSIONS AND REFLECTIONS

Although this chapter provides a teacher with strategies for defining problem behaviors, collecting data, and developing practical behavior change programs, it would be incomplete if consideration was not given to the purpose of the various management techniques described. Management for management's sake may result in a room full of children who are quietly completing nonstimulating tasks day after day. Docile and calm though they are, these children may have been trained to persist at tasks that do not challenge or actively engage them. As teachers, our task is to examine the content of our curriculum as carefully as we analyze behaviors in need of change (Winett & Winkler, 1972). With children who have been labeled as having special learning needs and who have been currently mainstreamed into a regular setting, it is especially important to focus on curricular as well as behavioral issues.

The content of a lesson may serve as an incentive for staying involved whether or not a child has difficulty in learning. The child who is very active and lacking in reading skills is more likely to be on-task when she is completing math problems using manipulative materials than when she faces a series of written work problems on a ditto. Specific strategies for increasing children's active participation in their own learning appear throughout this book. Successful classroom management depends upon integrating active learning experiences as much as it does on any data collection or incentive system.

QUESTIONS TO CONSIDER

1. Tape record a segment of your class day. How many of your comments are directed toward positive accomplishments? Can you increase this rate?
2. Select a child in your classroom who seems to "have your number." What specific behaviors does he or she have?
3. How could you measure these behaviors using guidelines presented in this chapter?
4. What would it look like if this child did what you would like him or her to do? What are the specific behaviors that you would like to see increased?
5. Select a child in your class whose behavior has improved. What are you doing differently? Based on information obtained in this chapter, what type of incentives are you using? Can you think of alternative incentives, perhaps more natural to the classroom?

5

Meeting the Special Learning
Needs of Each Child

When you work with elementary school children, part of your rewards grow from the fact that children are growing quickly and changing. Sometimes, just letting children "pass through" a difficult stage is
enough. They simply grow out of it. At other times, they need your
carefully planned intervention.

CASE STUDIES: GRADES 1, 2, 3, 4, and 6

In this chapter we want you to share the flavor of some carefully
planned teacher intervention programs through becoming acquainted
with five children. Each of the children had a problem that bothered
their teachers. For each child, the teacher spoke with somebody else,
looking for help. Then, the teacher worked out a curriculum plan and a
behavioral plan for the youngster.

JEFFREY: THE FLITTER (FIRST GRADE)

Dialogue with Parents

Ms. F. was an experienced early childhood teacher. She knew what
to expect from first graders, or at least she thought she did. The parent
conference, scheduled for her upcoming prep period, had raised
doubts in her mind about her understanding of young children's behavior. Jeffrey's parents had requested this meeting, almost as though they
had read her mind. She was eager to speak with them in hopes of
learning more about this six-year-old who never sat still!

Jeffrey's parents began their conference, "How can you stand up
after having had Jeffrey in your room all morning? Aren't you exhausted?" They proceeded to share with Ms. F. their reasons for com-

ing to school. "Jeffrey jumps from one thing to another, always touching something," shared his mother. "Usually the wrong things, too" added his father. "We wondered what you do that works so well with him."

Ms. F. smiled, at least partly in relief. She was glad that they felt she had some expertise that could be of assistance! She also hoped that they could shed some light on Jeffrey's behavior. "Let's look at this anecdotal observation I completed yesterday. It will give you an idea of some typical moments in Jeffrey's school day."

> Date: 9/14   Class activity: Children are
> Time begin: 9:00 a.m.   expected to copy sentences from
> Time end: 9:15 a.m.   the board into their notebooks.
>
> Jeffrey got up from his desk and walked away from the front of the room, toward the back, behind two other rows of desks. He stopped to say something to Meg, picked up a crayon piece from the floor, turned around, and headed toward the wastebasket in the front of the room. He threw out the crayon piece and walked toward his own seat. He stopped at the block corner, as he often does, to arrange yet another tower. After doing this he sat down at his own desk, reached into his school bag, and appeared to search for something. He rummaged around, removing two previous worksheets, an eraser, and leftover snacks. Finally he withdrew a stub of pencil. He returned the other items to the bag, dropped the bag, retrieved the bag, and replaced it on the back of his chair. He got up from his seat and proceeded toward the pencil sharpener—the long way around! He arrived at the sharpener, near the window, looked out the window, and then sharpened his already small pencil. He walked back toward his desk, via the front of my table, paused to look at a paperweight on the table and then proceeded to sit down in his own chair. Two minutes were spent looking through his desk for his notebook, which finally was taken out of the desk and placed in front of him. Fifteen minutes since the assignment had been given and Jeffrey was ready to begin!

Ms. F. explained to Jeffrey's parents that he was able to complete much of the assigned work provided that she stayed by his desk. He also loved spending time in the block area. As soon as she moved away and circulated among the other children, however, his wanderings would begin. She reported some success in getting him to return to his seat by "keeping at him" verbally whenever she saw him walking around the room. "The problem with this approach," she explained, "is that he gets right up again when I'm not looking."

Jeffrey's parents also had observed his "flitting behavior," but they were less concerned about it than they were about his "misbehavior." Both mother and father reported feeling great relief because their pediatrician and a consulting neurologist had ruled out "hyperactivity." Although the parents and Ms. F. were relieved to know that Jeffrey did not have a neurological problem, they were frustrated about his ability to "get into everything" regardless of the setting.

When asked by Ms. F. to describe a typical before-dinner scene with Jeffrey, they replied that they felt like drill sergeants most of the time. "You could hear us saying things like, 'Stop that, Jeffrey, you'll hurt the baby. No, not like that. Be careful with her rattle. No, don't touch the glass. Look out! You almost knocked it over.'"

Ms. F. thought to herself that it would be difficult for anyone to comply with that many directions in a one-minute period. Like so many parents of very active children, they had succumbed to the "command approach," which was far from successful.

Ms. F. realized that she, too, had a tendency to anticipate his unpleasant antics and to concentrate on his wanderings instead of on the occasional "good moments."

Curriculum Context/Prescription

When Jeffrey flits from place to place and activity to activity, his teacher's first impulse is to fantasy restraint, a quick-fix pill to make him stay put. Clearly, it is easy to notice his movement rather than the brief times when he settled on an activity for a few seconds. While Ms. F. can influence his staying power by ignoring or paying attention in a systematic way, she can use the broader curriculum context of a classroom to influence his behavior in a long-range view.

Jeffrey's teacher can adjust elements of the classroom's structure with a range of alternative choices in each of several areas discussed in chapters 1 and 2. In planning alternative choices, Ms. F. has become aware of recent research that identifies the need of some children who have high activity levels to create stimulation because they lack a sufficient level of inner stimulation (Koester and Farley, 1981). Often, these excessively active children create inappropriate stimulation, such as falling off chairs, racing around, and dropping things. Ms. F. is in a position to plan for stimulating activities and for varying the duration of activities. She can vary elements as follows:

Options—which activities and what content level
Pacing—when and for how long
Feedback—in relation to Jeffrey's progress, both in behavior and content achievement
Socialization—with whom Jeffrey can associate or near whom he might work best.

Options. His teacher planned separately for him when she noticed that Jeffrey spent his very few staying moments with concrete, manipulative materials such as blocks, puzzles, geoboards, and electric models, or in watching others use these activities, rather than paper-and-pencil tasks. She offered him choices between marking the arc of a pendulum or sorting into two baskets those objects that were or were not attracted by a magnet. In each activity, there was a need to record findings in order to compare his results with those found by other children. For example, in the magnet activity, he copied the labels attached to each object into two columns. Each activity was placed so that Jeffrey would work facing a wall in order to cut down visual distractions.

When she noticed that Jeffrey enjoyed looking at the *Curious George* (Rey) books, she developed a plan with him to create an advertising campaign to "sell" other children the pleasures of Curious George. Again, placing Jeffrey and poster-making materials facing toward a yellow room divider, Jeffrey had an opportunity to develop a bulletin board display without visual distractions.

Ms. F. added more concrete activities with which children needed to use skills such as drawing, reading, copying, writing, and arithmetic. She saw that when children had reasons to use and apply skills, they spent more time using their skills.

Pacing and Feedback. Ms. F. arranged for longer time blocks for the entire group to spend with activities. In that way, Jeffrey could have more chances to take more time at his work without interruptions or traffic involving the movement of the entire group.

The teacher spoke to Jeffrey and encouraged his work only when she was beside him but not when she was across the room. This was one way that she helped his concentration. She also spoke to other children directly in the areas in which they worked. In Jeffrey's case, Ms. F. commented, "You're really thinking about that one." "That's concentration!" "It's nice to see you working so carefully."

When Jeffrey did leave a planned activity, she ignored him, occasionally even turning her side to him. However, when he spent more than two minutes by the clock focused on an activity, she renewed her attention.

Socialization. Aside from watching other children from time to time, and touching objects that they were using, Jeffrey did not regularly seek out any particular children, nor did they seek his company. It occurred to Ms. F. that he might be stimulated to spend more time with an activity if it needed collaboration with another child. She planned to observe which other child she might pair with Jeffrey to carry on a survey of those adults in the school who smoked or did not smoke. They could then write up their findings as a bar graph. There were other cooperative mathematics activities that she foresaw for Jeffrey.

Behavioral Prescription

Defining the Problem. In the course of Ms. F.'s conference with Jeffrey's parents, she discovered several important issues related to her management of his classroom behavior. Unlike his parents, Ms. F. did not consider "misbehavior" to be his main problem. Her major concern was his flitting from task to task, which prevented him from exploring most of the learning activities in the classroom to any significant extent. She defined the problem as Jeffrey's inability to stay with most activities beyond several minutes. From her anecdotal observations she noted that Jeffrey frequently visited the block corner and stayed there as long as circumstances would allow.

Ms. F. also realized that she and Jeffrey's parents were likely to comment on the behaviors they did not wish to see much more than on the few times when Jeffrey worked constructively. Because she was uncertain both about how much Jeffrey flitted as well as how often he spent time in suitable activities, Ms. F. developed a system for gathering more information.

Collecting Data. Since Jeffrey's flitting behavior represented a type of off-task behavior, Ms. F. decided to keep track of instances of on-task and off-task behavior. Using momentary time sampling, described in chapter 4, Ms. F. observed Jeffrey for a few seconds at a time approximately ten times each morning and afternoon. Each time he was observed to be on-task (in the block corner if appropriate, copying labels, or doing sorting activities), he received a check. She computed a daily percentage of times when he was observed to be on-task. During the week before starting the action plan, Ms. F. was pleased to note that Jeffrey was on-task 40 percent of each morning and afternoon. There was hope after all!

Action Plans. Ms. F. used her observations to prompt her own comments to Jeffrey when he was working on an activity by himself or with other children. Ms. F. had learned that there was a much greater chance of Jeffrey staying with a task if it involved hands-on, inherently interesting materials than if it were simply a paper-and-pencil task. Knowing this, she became "ready" to comment quietly about his "working very hard," "trying," or "concentrating."

On those occasions when Jeffrey did flit or wander about, she ignored him but commented aloud about the fine job that Meg or John was doing.

During the first weeks of Ms. F.'s action plan, Jeffrey gradually built up his ability to stay with selected activities. As Ms. F. developed additional choices that "grabbed his interest," she noted more and more staying power in Jeffrey.

Ms. F. discovered that the most powerful incentive for Jeffrey was social approval. As Ms. F. had learned during her first weeks with Jeffrey and from his parents' comments, Jeffrey seldom had heard good things from the grownups around him. He seemed to thrive on the new found recognition that he and his classmates received for concentrating, cooperating, and completing tasks. Ms. F., in turn, was delighted with Jeffrey's eagerness to complete his Curious George poster. This was a far cry from the little boy who seldom stopped long enough to distinguish Curious George from Kermit the Frog.

FRANK: THE INVISIBLE CHILD (SECOND GRADE)

Dialogue with School Psychologist

MR. L.: I've tried everything with Frank. He's like a little mouse. Sometimes he's so quiet, I almost forget he's in my class.

DR. D.: Is Frank the little boy I've noticed on the sidelines when your class is at recess after lunch?

MR. L.: That's Frank, all right. At least he's watching the others . . . and sometimes Michelle joins him. They're both shy but Michelle does participate in classroom activities and she's a better student. Frank presents a dilemma for me because his shyness seems to affect his school work, too. He often leaves out answers on worksheets—or gets them wrong. When I sit with him, he's able to work better and, usually, he gets many more items correct.

DR. D.: How does he do during your Magic Circle time?

MR. L.: Not well at all. In fact, I've considered cutting back to two times a week because he seems so miserable during it. You know how the Magic Circle is supposed to work? The children have a chance to react to a question like, "What is your happiest time of day" or complete a sentence that begins with "I feel sad when. . . ." The sharing experiences lead to a nice discussion for most of us, even if it's only twenty minutes a day.

DR. D.: And how does Frank react to this?

MR. L.: He squirms in his seat, looks down at his feet, and says nothing when it's his turn. At first the other children would prod him to answer, but now they just ignore him. He looks as though he'd like

the floor to swallow him—which does nothing to make me feel better!

Dr. D.: Does Frank talk at home? I noticed his parents here at Open
School Night.

Mr. L.: They gave me some background information that was helpful
. . . to a point. It seems that Frank was a late talker and a very shy
little boy whenever he was around anyone outside the family. His
parents feel that he's more talkative now, although still quieter than
his ten-year-old and three-year-old sisters. His parents confessed
that they appreciated his quietness compared to the "noise" of his
sisters.

Dr. D.: What about his last year's teacher. Any help there?

Mr. L.: Last year and in kindergarten, Frank was described as a quiet,
rather slow child, who did make progress each year. Although
each teacher commented on his quietness, they didn't indicate any
negative effect on his social development.

I'm concerned about his becoming more and more of a
loner—and more behind in his school work. The other children
seem eager to work on projects together. Frank seems only eager
to work with me! I have the other twenty-three children to work with
as well.

Dr. D.: Are there any tasks he does independently?

Mr. L.: Not many. He does do some dittos, but with his limited reading
skills, he doesn't have many options when the others are doing
independent reading. I've been trying to think of activities that
would involve him in the group more but I don't want to over-
whelm him.

Curriculum Context/Prescription

Frank might just as well be invisible or not in school at all for the
impact he has on the classroom. His teacher, Mr. L., felt as if he was
playing hide-and-go-seek with Frank and had not yet found the child.
However, Mr. L. did feel that he was beginning to see a shadowy image.
His major concerns were to build some academic success experience for
Frank and to increase Frank's involvement with other children.

Options.   With poor reading skills, Frank needed a variety of materials that demanded a simple reading level. During the independent work
time, Frank was able to build models and place preprinted word labels
on the parts. He was given thematic word-find puzzles and simple cloze
exercises as well as opportunities to draw pictures related to the word-

find puzzles and cloze exercises, for example, indoor pictures, farm pictures, pet antics.

Mr. L. ordered the Scholastic (Scholastic School Services, 1984) tape recordings and books program. Until the material arrived, he tape recorded several picture books that included repetitive text and picture context clues, such as *Caps for Sale* (Slobodkin), *The Noisy Book* (Brown), and *Ask Mr. Bear* (Flack). With an earphone, Frank would listen to the story, following the text in the book.

Frank could use precut strips of oaktag to measure the equivalent lengths of a limited number of objects in the classroom. Attached to each object were preprinted labels that he could copy next to the lengths of oaktag strips on a large chart. Other children would add their findings.

Pacing and Feedback. Mr. L. provided short-range activities in which he had controlled the new variables with which Frank would need to cope. As Frank approached his short-term work, Mr. L. demonstrated the new variable and modelled the format to follow in each activity in order to help Frank complete the task. Beginning with very brief tasks, Mr. L. was able to let Frank know how well he had done to complete the activity. In turn, the scope of subsequent tasks was extended. Whenever Frank completed the new extended work, Mr. L. was able to give Frank feedback concerning how well he was completing more complex work: "Remember when you were doing six problems? Now you are finishing eleven of these more difficult problems."

Socialization. Mr. L. set up a number of activities that required Frank to work with one or more children. Using controlled variables, there was a concentration game with simple consonant-vowel-consonant word patterns, such as bat: bit; fat: fit; hat: hit; sat: sit. Michelle was one of the other children, along with one or two others, whom the teacher encouraged to play together. With similar controlled variables, Mr. L. developed a Go-Fish card game in which children needed to ask one another if they held a matching card. Knowing that these second graders were just beginning to hold cards in a fan, Mr. L. partially sawed several 1" × 1" strips of wood to serve as card stands.

Mr. L. offered Frank and a more outgoing child the chance to prepare a puppet show, using one of Frank's favorite storybooks as the theme. Frank and the other child had the choice of tape recording their dialogue or presenting it "live" after practice sessions.

In another activity, Frank and Michelle planned with each other what questions they could ask when interviewing the local postmaster. They had already witnessed interviews with other community workers and merchants conducted by other children in the class as part of an oral history project. By working with only one other child at a time, Frank had a chance to feel more comfortable than he had been in the larger group setting. Pairing in these ways may be a precursor to his progress in coping with larger group settings.

Behavioral Prescription

Defining the Problem.   Frank's inability to work independently and his excessive shyness were Mr. L.'s main concerns. He was pleased with the initial results of his curricular changes for Frank. With a greater variety of tasks at his success level, Frank was completing more and more work on his own.

Collecting Data.   Mr. L. had begun to collect information about Frank's classroom accomplishments before actually implementing any of the new projects for Frank. Using the permanent product system, described in chapter 4, Mr. L. counted the number of problems completed or questions answered independently by Frank.

Based upon that first week's observations, Frank completed 20 percent of his work during independent work time. With the introduction of tasks such as model building, word-find puzzles, and listening to pre-recorded stories, Frank's completed activities rose to 75–80 percent.

Action Plan.   Mr. L.'s concerns about Frank's shyness and social isolation lessened as Frank became more involved with Michelle and several other children who worked together on class projects. Initially Mr. L. had counted the number of times that Frank initiated any comments to Michelle while they worked together. When he noticed that Michelle did all the initiating, Mr. L. developed a new plan. He set up a game situation with Frank and Michelle and carefully explained the rules. "In this Go-Fish game, you score a point by asking your partner if she or he has a card you need. If your partner has to remind you, you do not get any points." As expected, Frank caught on!

Mr. L. was careful to make many specific positive statements throughout the day regarding Frank's independent work, his cooperative projects, and his newly discovered talking talent.

WILMA: THE THIRD-GRADE TERROR

Dialogue with Principal

"I have had it!" exclaimed Ms. R. to the principal, Ms. C. "That child is destroying my class, and my peace of mind in the process." Ms. R.

was describing Wilma, a taller than average student in her third-grade classroom. "It's not that she is a slow student. In fact, even if I call on her in the middle of a scuffle, she's likely to give the correct answer." Ms. C. listened before asking Ms. R. for a more specific description of Wilma's behavior.

Ms. R.: Wilma is trouble waiting to happen! A trip to the wastebasket is apt to result in two other children complaining that Wilma stepped on their feet or grabbed their papers. If I speak to Wilma about this, she insists that it's not her fault.

Ms. C.: Have you contacted her parents or spoken to her previous teachers?

Ms. R.: Last week I arranged a conference with her parents. They're concerned about her "bad temper" but they don't have any specific system for dealing with it. They said they were inconsistent. They use everything from threats to spanking and sending her to her room for hours. Lately they've begun to advise their other children to keep clear of Wilma when she's in one of her moods. They're cooperative parents but they don't have much to offer in the way of suggestions.

Ms. C.: What about her other teacher? I don't remember that Wilma was such a problem before.

Ms. R.: I looked at her records the other day. She started kindergarten as a pretty bright child, "precocious" is what Mr. G. used to describe her. In first and second grade, the teachers commented more and more about her "lack of respect" and occasional "bullying." She still came across as being bright. She seems to be getting worse each year.

Ms. C.: Why don't I visit your class tomorrow and observe Wilma in action? At least I'll know first-hand what you're facing. Maybe another perspective will help us develop a plan for making you and Wilma feel better.

As Ms. C. arrived in Ms. R.'s classroom, Wilma was walking toward the water fountain.

PAULA: You stepped on my foot, Wilma.

WILMA: I did not. You stuck it out on purpose.

Ms. R.: Stop it, children, this minute! Wilma, sit down on your own chair! All right, let's continue talking about all these materials. Who knows what this is? (Teacher holds up the partially dirt- and plant-filled fish tank.) Joanne, do you know?

JOANNE: A fish tank?

WILMA: That's dumb. It's a terrarium.

Ms. R.: Wilma, it's not nice to call someone dumb. What else are we going to put in our terrarium?

CASEY: That lizard over there?

Ms. R.: That's right Casey, this lizard . . . but this lizard has a special name. Who remembers from yesterday? (three children, including Wilma, raise their hands.) Jenni, what is it called?

JENNI: A samanander. (Several children giggle.)

WILMA: A salamander, Jenni, remember the *l* sound.

Ms. R.: That's right, girls, it's a salamander. Can anyone tell me what other animal looks something like a salamander? (No immediate response from the children. Wilma sighs out loud and mumbles something.)

Ms. R.: What was that, Wilma?

WILMA: A chameleon and a newt. Who doesn't know that?

JENNI AND CASEY: Don't act so smart all the time.

Ms. R.: That's enough children. Patrick, let's put some moss over here. (Wilma is seen pushing into Jenni, and leaning her elbow against Casey. They tell her to stop in loud whispers.)

Ms. R.: All right, Wilma, you've asked for it! Go back to your seat and stay there until we finish this. Does anyone know what's special about sala- manders, chameleons, and newts? (Several children raise their hands. Their answers are correct facts, such as, they eat insects, they sneak up on their prey, but the responses apparently are not what Ms. R. wants. Wilma is mumbling again.)

WILMA: Bunch of babies. Don't even know about camouflage. We heard about that on the field trip last year.

Ms. R.: You're not in this group, Wilma. Keep doing your spelling words . . . four times each.

Curriculum Context/Prescription

In a short time, Wilma's teacher and the other children in her class learned to keep their distance from Wilma and to tiptoe gingerly with her when they could not avoid contact. Ms. R., Wilma's teacher, felt that she could find relief if only Wilma did not disrupt group discussions and if she could keep her busy enough during work periods so that she would not disturb other children.

Options.   First, Ms. R. and Ms. C. reviewed the written record of the class's terrarium discussion. Ms. R. noticed that Wilma did slip in occasional valuable comments but that Ms. R., herself, was so busy keeping up her guard that she did not react except with a second of relief. She needed to watch for more chances to provide appreciation.

After reviewing the questions that the principal pointed out, Ms. R. began to wonder if she had not been asking too many fact-stating and "what" kinds of questions. She planned to add more questions that required children to make comparisons, to relate events, and to focus more on "whys." Since Wilma was highly verbal and seemed bright, Ms. R. hoped that the higher-level questions would help to focus Wilma's energy in a more positive direction rather than on scathing comments about other children. It also occurred to her that Wilma might appreciate reading *Much Ado About Aldo* (Hurwitz) in which a boy in third grade considers some profound questions as an outgrowth of a terrarium project similar to the one in their class.

Second, when she began to consider the work period, her first impulse was to send Wilma to work in the computer center since she was able and it would remove Wilma from the classroom. Ms. R. realized that the computer center placement only postponed dealing with the problem when the child returned. Nevertheless, Ms. R. felt that she would give herself the half hour of relief each day to recharge her own energy level.

Ms. R. planned to ask Wilma to deal more with relational questions, such as, "Why would camouflage be important to an animal? In what ways can people use camouflage? When have you seen a person camouflage her feelings?"

She arranged to give Wilma a set of filmstrips on the food cycle and put Wilma's name on the list of children who would study mealworms. She would help Wilma and a subgroup of other bright-but-strong children relate terrains and water sources with different cultures. In the past, she had found such activities led to the study of comparative life styles in different regions and into multicultural education. A good reader, two stanines above grade level, Wilma would be able to read and report about her comparisons. There would also be opportunities to develop charts and relief models to share with the larger group.

Pacing and Feedback.

When Wilma was stimulated by challenging activity, she could be expected not to disturb others. Ms. R. recognized that, rather than relaxing with relief when Wilma was appropriately occupied, she needed to pay attention to signs of Wilma's transition times, when Wilma was closing down her involvement and needed additional stimulation. At those moments, Ms. R. made it a point to help Wilma consider ways to extend her work and raised questions concerning possible activities that would follow.

Also, as the teacher circulated among the children who were engaged in independent individual and small-group activities, she took note of moments when Wilma was working cooperatively and commented, "It's nice to see you planning so carefully together."

Socialization. Ms. R. was concerned that other children in the class might change from simply avoiding Wilma to using her as a scapegoat. Therefore, she tried to speak privately to Wilma when there was behavior that could not be ignored.

The teacher suggested that Wilma pair off with another child who was well-liked in order to prepare together a dramatization for presentation to the class. They needed to review and compare the possibilities for dramatizing scenes from among ten books that they had read between them. Both advanced readers, this activity provided a challenge for Wilma and her partner. The activity culminated in a prestigious, very funny presentation to the entire class. While hardly a panacea, this activity permitted the children to see Wilma in a more approachable way. At the very least, there was a positive experience that was shared in common.

Behavioral Prescription

Defining the Problem. Ms. R. was on the right track when she realized that Wilma did occasionally make relevant contributions to the class. In order to increase her own awareness of the times when Wilma was involved appropriately in class activities, Ms. R. planned to collect more systematic information about Wilma's on-task behavior.

Collecting Data. Using the momentary time sampling model, described in chapter 4, Ms. R. developed a data collection sheet that allowed her to observe Wilma unobtrusively several times each morning and afternoon. She would look at Wilma for a few seconds to determine whether or not she was working cooperatively or was involved in a task. Placing a check mark in the appropriate square, Ms. R. was able to keep track of a daily percentage of Wilma's on-task behavior.

Initially Wilma appeared to be involved in meaningful activity 40 percent of the times she was observed. After Ms. R. put her curriculum plans into effect, Wilma became involved in a number of stimulating projects and the percentage gradually increased to between 70 and 80 percent each day. Clearly progress was being made!

Ms. R. also had kept track of Wilma's physical acting out by keeping a daily tally of the number of times she hit or pushed someone. This type of observation system, event recording, was described in detail in chapter 4. Ms. R. noted that Wilma averaged eight to ten incidents weekly before she changed the curriculum, increased her own positive comments for Wilma's productive behavior, and used time-out (see the next section, Action Plans). After implementing these procedures, Wilma's physical aggression decreased rapidly. Within several weeks, Wilma's hitting and pushing were almost a thing of the past. The incidents occurred no more than twice in two weeks.

Action Plans.   Ms. R.'s efforts to voice her appreciation of Wilma's sharing, researching, and questioning behaviors were well rewarded. Wilma basked in her new limelight.

The problem remained of dealing with Wilma's infrequent but still occurring hitting incidents. Clearly, hitting or physically hurting anyone is behavior that cannot be tolerated in a classroom. Consultation with the principal and school psychologist resulted in a technique called time-out.

Any time Wilma, or any other student for that matter, hit or pushed another child she was immediately directed to the time-out carrel placed in the left-hand corner of the classroom. Within easy access of Ms. R.'s desk, it was off the beaten track of the various interest areas.

Time-out is a time away from positive happenings in the classroom. Neutral and boring would be apt descriptions of the time-out setting. Neither teacher nor other children interact with a child who is in time-out. Experience has shown that a *brief* period away from the incentives provided in the classroom setting is effective in stopping the inappropriate behavior. Time-out works best when it follows immediately after a specific, forbidden behavior.

For Wilma, it was especially helpful to introduce the time-out technique at the same time that the environment was becoming more stimulating and positive for her. Wilma previously had enjoyed the attention that her bullying had provided. She had not met the same level of success in any other experience in the classroom. Once the classroom situation had changed for Wilma and she was receiving positive feedback from teacher and children alike, she did not enjoy being removed from it, for even the required five-minute time-out interval.

JULIE, THE UNFAMILIAR (FOURTH GRADE)

Dialogue in the Principal's Office

Ms. L.: You can't mean that I'm going to have a child who uses a wheelchair in my classroom! I'm not a special education teacher!

Mr. D.: No, you're not a special education teacher . . . you're a fine fourth-grade teacher who's worked well with hundreds of children for over ten years. Let me tell you a little about Julie and then we'll discuss the appropriate place for her.

Julie has a type of cerebral palsy, spastic diplegia in medical jargon. For Julie, this means that her legs and parts of her arms do not respond to brain messages the way our limbs do. She uses a wheelchair for longer distances but she can manage to get from her wheelchair to her desk, or to work tables around the classroom by using her crutches.

She's been tested often, as you can imagine, and she has at least average ability. Her reading is somewhat above grade level, while her math is somewhat below. She speaks well—and often! The reports received from the school district she's leaving have commented on her strong verbal skills and her perseverance. She had been "mainstreamed" in that district during third grade and apparently did well.

Ms. L.: How did she get along with other children? Wasn't there a lot of teasing and staring? Who helped her get around?

Mr. D.: Whoa! Slow down! Let's take one step at a time. I suggest we invite Julie and her parents to meet with us later this week. By then we'll have had a chance to organize our main concerns and to see how well our building and classrooms can accommodate a child who uses a wheelchair and crutches.

Julie and her parents arrived at the principal's office Thursday afternoon. "This is a neat building," was Julie's first comment upon meeting Mr. D. Ms. L. smiled at Julie and extended her hand. "Welcome to Taylor School." After introductions, the group met in Mr. D.'s office for an hour. Ms. L. had prepared several questions for Julie and her parents.

Physical education and management of the building was a major priority for this teacher. When Julie was asked about her experiences in gym class, she responded quickly, "That's what everyone wants to know! My last year's teacher showed me how to play softball with the other kids. The ball is on a tee and I bat it. Somebody else runs for me . . . a pinch runner I think it's called."

Mr. D. and Ms. L. had spoken with the physical education teacher in their building and offered another idea. "Have you tried bowling with Indian pins?" Julie replied that she hadn't but would like to learn as many games as possible.

Julie's parents shared with Ms. L. and Mr. D. their belief that although physical education was an important part of Julie's school experience, it was an aspect that could be developed gradually as they worked together. Mr. D. agreed, saying that their physical education teacher had mentioned a number of books that described activities that would be fun and beneficial to Julie and other fourth graders as well.

Fire drills and toileting issues were quickly resolved. Since Julie used a wheelchair in the corridors and outdoors, she would get into her chair at the sound of the fire bell. Ms. L. or a classmate would push Julie to the nearest exit. Mr. D. mentioned that he would alert the fire department about Julie, just as he would about any child who used crutches and/or a wheelchair.

Toileting was an activity that Julie said was no problem for her. She uses her wheelchair to get there and then uses her crutches once inside.

Lunchroom and recess were the last physical management issues raised by Ms. L. "When I'm in my chair, I can go through the line like anyone else. I might need help reaching for the food but another kid could do that for me," Julie replied.

"Oh, Julie, one more question. What should I do if you fall in the classroom?" "Well," said Julie, "I do need help getting up. My arms aren't as strong as I'd like. You could put your arms under my arms and sort of help me up."

Ms. L. was becoming more impressed with Julie's positive attitude by the minute. She realized that many of her concerns had grown out of a lack of experience with anyone who had a major physical disability. At this point in the conversation, Ms. L. felt, for the first time, that she could discuss the curriculum, the classroom, and adjustment to new classmates with Julie and her parents as she would with any new student entering her class in November.

Curriculum Context/Prescription

Once Ms. L. and other school people got beyond viewing Julie as if she were an invader from another planet, to see the person behind the hardware, they were able to focus on her academic work. As Ms. L. planned with Julie, she came to trust Julie's ability to direct ways of working.

Options. With decent reading skills, Julie easily fit into a reading group using grade-level skills. Her writing was done most comfortably in a notebook with a firm cover clipped on a clipboard. These provisions anticipated her irregular coordination.

Julie needed extra help in mathematics and could use additional concrete materials. Ms. L. found trays with high edges on which Julie could work with concrete materials. The high edges kept items contained so that a sudden movement would not scatter them. Centimeter-size graph paper was helpful in aligning numbers for arithmetic problems.

Eventually, Ms. L. would use Julie's verbal strength in teaching her long division by the use of divide, multiply, subtract, and bring down (Margaret Haesloop, personal communication, 1983).

Pacing and Feedback. Ms. L. expected that Julie would be slower in physical activities and that she would have to keep aware and try to anticipate the child's needs. Ms. L. recognized that rushing any child could make that child feel less adequate. At the same time, Ms. L. was anxious to provide Julie with encouragement and appreciation when the child made academic progress and showed initiative.

Socialization. It was important that the other children come to see Julie as a competent peer in the classroom. Building on Julie's verbal strength, Ms. L. invited Julie to be part of a small role-playing group. The role-playing group began their work along guidelines presented in Shaftel and Shaftel, *Role Playing for Social Values* (1967). They were planning to develop a chart and narrated presentation for the rest of the class.

After role playing alternative solutions to a social problem, the children in this group would settle on one solution and present their improvisational role playing to the remainder of the class.

The science program was another natural contact with an ongoing small group of children. Several children worked together in manipulating materials and recording their findings, using the Elementary Science Study unit on pendulums (McGraw-Hill, 1976). They were planning to develop a chart and narrated presentation for the rest of the class.

Ms. L. expected that the small informal social studies and science groups would help to build toward spontaneous contacts that could spill over into lunch and recess.

Behavioral Prescription

Introduction. Ms. L. anticipated that Julie, as any newcomer, might need assistance in becoming an active part of her new fourth grade classroom. Her physical disability added to the task, since Ms. L. felt that the children may be as inexperienced as she had been when it came to working with someone who uses a wheelchair and crutches.

Looking back two weeks, when she had first been told that Julie might join her class, Ms. L. remembered that all she could think about were Julie's "appliances." After becoming acquainted with Julie, however, and discovering her to be a competent, personable fourth grader, she could move on to concerns related to any newcomer.

Ms. L. began her class's preparation for Julie with the routine announcement that a new child soon would join them. She said that the new student's name was Julie, that she and her family recently had moved from Massachusetts, and that Julie had a pet dog. After this introduction, Ms. L. mentioned that Julie used an interesting method to get around, specifically a wheelchair and crutches. After answering several questions about why Julie used a wheelchair and crutches, Ms. L. asked the class to help her check the classroom for obstacles or barriers that might make it difficult for Julie to move around with ease.

Ms. L. planned to include her class actively in preparing for Julie after having read *What's the Difference? Teaching Positive Attitudes Toward People with Disabilities* (Barnes, Berrigan, & Bilken, 1978). Included in this book is a checklist for assessing architecture barriers (see figure 5.1).

After checking their classroom, the bathroom, corridors, and building grounds, Ms. L.'s students were satisfied that only minor adjustments were necessary in their classroom. They moved the art supplies to lower shelves and they asked Mr. Frank, the school custodian, to raise the height of one of their work tables so that Julie's wheelchair could fit comfortably under it.

When Julie arrived at Room 18 the next week, she found a group of children waiting to say hello before they entered the classroom. Ms. L. smiled at Julie and the welcoming committee, once again remembering her initial anxiety over Julie's assignment to her class.

During the weeks preceding and following Julie's arrival, Ms. L.'s students asked a number of questions about Julie's wheelchair and physical disabilities in general. Several children wanted to try out the crutches and wheelchair, which they did.

While Julie could answer many questions, there were many others that neither she nor Ms. L. could handle. The school librarian and the district's special education office had several books, filmstrips, and guest speakers to send to Ms. L.'s classroom. (A list of suggested books and audiovisual materials appear at the end of this chapter.)

Defining the Problem.   Although Julie's physical and academic integration into Room 18 appeared to be going smoothly, Ms. L. was concerned about her progress in becoming an active member of the class, of truly "belonging" to Room 18. She defined the specific behaviors that she was interested in as initiating activities with other students and being asked to join activities by others.

Collecting Data.   She chose event recording as a data collection system. She noted both how often Julie initiated contact with other

Figure 5.1 Barriers Checklist

	Barrier free	
If the main entrance to the school has a ramp it is barrier free. If it has stairs, and no ramp, it has a barrier.	Yes	No
Are the door knobs of all main doors three feet from the ground so that people in wheelchairs can reach them?	Yes	No
Do the hallways have handrails to help people walk? No handrails is a barrier for some people.	Yes	No
Parking Spaces: Are there parking spaces reserved for disabled people? Are they near the entrance of the building? Are they 12 feet wide? Are there at least 2 out of every 100 spaces reserved for people who have disabilities?	Yes	No
Are there curb cuts so that people in wheelchairs, or people with baby carriages or shopping carts can pass easily?	Yes	No
Are there tactile markings (can be felt by touch) cut in the sidewalk to warn people who are blind?	Yes	No
If your school has more than one floor, does it have an elevator? (Skip this question if your school is one floor.)	Yes	No
Does the elevator have braille markers for the floor buttons? (Skip this question if your school is one floor.)	Yes	No

Note: Reprinted with permission from Barnes, E., Berrigan, C., & Biklen, D., What's the difference? Teaching positive attitudes toward people with disabilities (Syracuse, N.Y.: Human Policy Press, 1978), 81-83.

132

Figure 5.1 (Continued)

	Barrier free	
Does the elevator have light and bell signals to help people who are blind or deaf to know when the elevator is ready? (Skip this question if your school is one floor.)	Yes	No
Are the doorways to all bathrooms at least 33 inches wide?	Yes	No
Are your sinks low enough? Get a chair and see if you can reach the sink while you're sitting in the chair. If not, then the sinks will probably be unusable for people in wheelchairs.	Yes	No
Are the telephones in the building accessible? Use the same test as for the sinks. How many inches should they be lowered?	Yes	No
Are the fire alarms low enough for people in wheelchairs?	Yes	No
Are there grab bars in the bathroom stalls so that people can lift themselves from a wheelchair to the toilet and back again?	Yes	No
Are the windows 24 inches or 28 inches from the floor so that short people and people in wheelchairs can see out?	Yes	No
Are the aisles in the classroom at least 32 inches wide so that people in wheelchairs, or on crutches, or with canes or walkers, can get around easily?	Yes	No
Are there flashing lights for fire alarms so that deaf students will know if there's a fire?	Yes	No

133

Figure 5.1   (Continued)

                                      Barrier free

Are there picture signs to show the purpose of each   Yes   No

room so that people who cannot read will know where

to go?

Count up the number of Yes answers. Total Yes answers_____

Count up the number of No answers. Total No answers_____

Here is how to figure out whether your school gets a passing grade or not:

$$\frac{\text{Multiply Number of Yes Answers X 100}}{18} = \underline{\hspace{3cm}}\%$$

70% is a passing score.

---

children and how often she was chosen to participate in a group during each morning for a two-week period. Figure 5.2 presents a sample weekly recording system which fits on a 3×5 note card. Ms. L. placed a mark in the appropriate column whenever she observed Julie going to or being asked to join a group.

Action Plans.   It became apparent that Julie was doing fine with regard to approaching the other students but that her classmates were somewhat reluctant to ask her to join them. As indicated in the preceding section, Ms. L. combined group process with academic tasks in the role-playing and science activities. Ms. L. had delayed starting these groups until after she had collected data about Julie's socialization. Ms. L. decided to assign Julie initially to those groups of students who had approached Julie when she first arrived at Taylor School.

As Julie worked cooperatively with these two groups of students, Ms. L. had many opportunities to comment positively about their concentration, their commitment to the tasks, and their ability to work well together. Ms. L.'s feedback to the group as well as their successful experience of working together resulted in a natural incentive system: social approval and self-reinforcement.

Like Julie, Karen, who is introduced in the next section, also faces a socialization problem. Their teachers have similar concerns about planning learning activities in ways that help them become accepted group members in order to avoid group disruption, scapegoating, or ostracism. These considerations become especially obvious when children from special classes spend part of their time in regular classrooms. Some examples in chapter 6 provide further details of ways that teachers have implemented Individual Education Plans (IEP) in these areas.

KAREN: THE ZINGER (SIXTH GRADE)

Dialogue in the Teachers' Room

Scene: Teacher's lounge during lunch. Several teachers are eating lunch and talking with Ms. J., a sixth grade teacher.

Ms. J.: That Karen is always starting something! Again and again, she goes after the children's weak spots. No wonder she hasn't any friends.

Ms. H.: What sets her off?

Ms. J.: It could be anything. Let me tell you what happened this morning. We were discussing our usual current events assignment and Karen called out repeatedly without raising her hand. When I called on Joey, who had raised his hand, she pouted and began mumbling under her breath. Poor Joey, his face is starting to break out, and Karen called out, "Joey-the-leopard, covered with spots!" Joey turned red and told Karen to "shut up."

Ms. H.: She sounds like a nasty child. Does she have any good points?

Ms. J.: That's the funny thing. When I've kept Karen after school, she's a different person. She chats with me about television shows and

Figure 5.2   Sample Event Recording Form for Julie

Days	Initiates Activity		Joins Activity
Mon	///		/
Tues	//		0
Wed	//		/
Thurs	///		//
Fri	/		0
Total	11		4

newspaper stories. She asks if she can help me correct papers or
water plants.

Ms. H.: Sounds like a regular Jekyll and Hyde. Seriously, have you
checked out her home situation? Maybe she's got problems there
you don't know about.

Ms. J.: They're as baffled as I am. I spoke with them last week, after a
particularly trying day, and they were glad I had called. They
described her as being "fresh" much of the time, especially since
beginning puberty this past summer. Dinner time has become a
nightmare for them. Karen apparently squabbles with her two
younger sisters and challenges every statement that her parents
make. They feel that she has become sensitive and self-conscious
about her physical development.

Ms. R.: Has she had problems before? I vaguely remember her name
being mentioned by Mr. L. last year.

Ms. J.: Her marks have been "average" throughout the grades but all
the teachers commented that she seemed capable of doing much
better. There were no special difficulties mentioned. I spoke with
Mr. L. and he said that Karen had begun to speak out and "clown
around" in his class toward the end of the year.

Ms. H.: Maybe she has emotional problems and should be in a smaller
class?

Ms. J.: I'd have thought the same thing except for the change in her
whenever she meets with me alone or occasionally when she's talking with some of the first and second graders on the playground
before school. She hasn't noticed me looking, thank goodness.
She seems almost motherly when she asks them about their pets
or their lunches or just about anything. If I could only channel her
good points.

Curriculum Context/Prescription

Karen's stings hurt other children. They blush, bluster, shrink,
stammer, and curse. Somehow, she manages to find everybody's weakest
spot. Ms. J., her teacher, thought that if Karen felt better about herself,
she might have less need to put down others. Ms. J. felt that she needed
to be better able to anticipate when Karen might strike since this was
Karen's way to distract other children from being one-up on her. She felt
that Karen needed more sense of academic competence as well as social
acceptance. Ms. J. saw academic success as one way for Karen to feel
more powerful.

Options. Since Karen happily discussed politics with her teacher after school, Ms. J. suggested that Karen might enjoy selecting a political article from the local newspapers each day for display on the "News-of-the-Day" bulletin board. This activity required scanning two newspapers, reading, selecting an article, hanging it, and writing a challenging question as a caption.

Karen, with another child, also conducted political research surveys among adults who worked in the school. They planned a questionnaire each week based upon their review of the newspapers, focusing in turn on local, state, national, and international issues. The children recorded their findings on a bar graph and reported to part of the class. Self-consciousness about her physical development still caused Karen to shy away from reporting to the entire class.

When these results, some of which reflected attitudes toward controversial issues, helped some children see Karen in a more acceptable frame, Ms. J. arranged for some role playing of social problems, following the Shaftel format (Shaftel & Shaftel, 1967). Using large photographs as a stimulus, children define a problem and then role play alternate solutions, changing roles. In this way, Karen had the chance to play the role of a victim as well as an aggressor.

Pacing and Feedback. In addition to these collaborative projects, Ms. J. believed that Karen might be able to achieve more in her skills. She arranged for Karen to choose two areas of study in mathematics and in composition that involved a contract format. Karen chose to do decimals, and percentages related to money and interest, an outgrowth of her concern about politics. She also chose exercises in composition that involved editing by reducing the number of words. Karen and Ms. J. began with shorter contracts. As Karen completed each one, Ms. J. would give her special attention and asked Karen to set up new, longer contracts that made increasing, yet reasonable demands. For example, in three days, Karen felt that she could complete three sections of math problems and one reduction of a 1,200-word printed passage to 800 words.

With other activities, Ms. J. planned with Karen and made a personal list of activities that she could do independently when she finished her contracted work each day, such as read a trade book, add to the class's communal latch hook rug (two latch hooks), reach into the "free time" grab bag for a surprise activity, write a limerick, or record findings with the pendulum using a task card. In this way, she felt that Karen would gain a needed sense of control over some of her time in school and would be more willing to fit into more tightly scheduled group activities.

Socialization.   Ms. J. built collaborative opportunities into Karen's academic work on a regular basis. She also felt that Karen needed some help in understanding her own pubescence. She arranged a meeting with Karen's mother at which these issues were discussed and Ms. J. suggested some readings that Karen might do at home and at school with parental permission. Among them were *Blubber* (Blume, 1976), *Harriet the Spy* (Fitzhugh, 1964), and *I Know You, Al* (Greene, 1975). Ms. J. also suggested that Karen's parents might read *Between Parent and Teenager* (Ginnot, 1969), which suggests a stock of ways in which parents can perceive their children's feelings and become more positive in dealing with them.

Behavioral Prescription

Defining the Problem.   Ms. J. saw Karen's need to feel better about herself. She continued her after-school discussions with Karen as she put into practice the various curricular changes. Karen certainly had fewer outbursts and was becoming more likeable the more she became involved in class activities.

Collecting Data.   Ms. J. had collected information about Karen's angry outbursts since the third week of school. She devised a simple tally system, event recording, as described in chapter 4.

The news was not encouraging as she reviewed the daily tallies for the past month. Karen "blew-up" and made fun of someone in the class between two and four times each day! The outbursts had declined to fewer than one per day in the two weeks since beginning the curriculum activities.

Action Plans.   Ms. J. wanted Karen to have as much responsibility as possible in developing a plan to stop the noisy disruptions. Capitalizing on her good after-school relationship with Karen, Ms. J. shared her concerns with Karen. She showed the daily tallies to her and asked her if she wanted to begin a "self-control" project. Karen mentioned that she did not like to be a troublemaker but she didn't know how to stop. Ms. J. had done some reading, suggested by the school psychologist, prior to this meeting and was able to explain to Karen that there were some techniques that they could practice together that would help Karen develop more self-control (Meichenbaum, 1977).

Karen agreed to try and asked if she could continue to meet with Ms. J. to work on the project. Ms. J. developed a system with Karen that began to shift the responsibility for recording information to Karen. They devised a form such as the one in figure 5.3.

After several days of completing these logs, Karen noticed that she tended to get angry when (1) she felt that Ms. J. paid more attention to other students in the class than to her and (2) when she made mistakes on her work. Ms. J. and Karen practiced the "deep breathing" recommended as a way to calm down. They also discussed some of the things that Karen could say to herself to change the discouraged or annoyed feelings she was experiencing prior to an outburst. Examples of these included:

"I'm doing much better at controlling my temper now than before."

"My work is improving and that makes me feel proud."

"Everyone makes mistakes sometimes. At least I have a chance to correct them."

"There are a lot of kids in this room and Ms. J. has to spend time with them, too."

After several weeks, Karen and Ms. J. were happy with the results. Karen's daily logs showed fewer and fewer "angry feelings." Her pride in her accomplishments was obvious when she said to Ms. J., "I guess it is pretty mature to solve some of your own problems."

SUMMARY

This chapter described the cases of five children who presented problems in their respective classrooms. For each child, a curriculum

Figure 5.3 Child-maintained Feelings Log for Karen

Day: _____			
I felt angry when	I took 3 deep breaths yes	no	Then I did

plan as well as behavioral plan was presented to deal with flitting from task to task, shyness, bullying, disruptiveness, and a physical disability.

Curriculum planning was assisted when teachers used a framework for (1) defining options by examining existing activities and the content level of each activity; (2) regulating pacing by deciding which activity should occur when and for how long; (3) supplying feedback by letting the children know how they are doing in achievement and in behavior; and (4) socially integrating the child by observing the child and making decisions about seating and work arrangements.

Behavioral management was assisted when teachers used a framework for (1) defining the problem by focusing on the specific behavior(s) they would like to see increased or decreased; (2) collecting data by observing specific behaviors and counting them, usually by means of event recording, permanent products, or momentary time sampling; and (3) devising specific action plans, noting which incentives should be used for which behaviors.

Sometimes children shared in their own data collection. Usually, they were involved in selecting options and pacing themselves. Throughout this chapter, teachers consulted with various other significant adults in their students' lives: building principal, school psychologist, parents, and former teachers. Information from all sources led to creative, more effective curriculum and behavior management.

We recommend that you keep these simple frameworks in mind as you plan for behavioral change and improved academic performance. As you adapt the frameworks to your own teaching situation, they can serve to help sharpen your view of your own teaching alternatives.

CONCLUSIONS AND REFLECTIONS

Genes notwithstanding, you, the teacher, continue to face your Jeffrey, your Frank, your Wilma, your Julie, and your Karen tomorrow. Even with the most cooperative parents and help from home (or the reverse), they are yours to deal with tomorrow. Even with last year's teacher agreeing that Wilma is downright fresh and disrespectful, it is of little use to your actions to say, "I'm right. See, this other teacher also found the same thing. It's not my fault." This can translate too subtly into, "It's not my responsibility to try to undo." Even if you discover poor achievement in the past and low reading scores, it is of little use to your plans to say, "What can I do!? After all, he has a low reading level."

Perpetuating other teachers' stereotypes and low expectations tend to add to your sense of burden because you are where the buck has stopped. Yet, there is hope. Other teachers have found relief by using some of the alternatives described in this chapter. They are variables to consider, try out, and adapt to your situation.

These alternatives exist in managing behavior and in managing curriculum. In a nutshell, children need to hear from you clearly and consistently what is allowed and what are the limits for your classroom. Even if school-wide guidelines may be ambiguous or absent, you need to clearly communicate your own limits and to provide plenty of positive appreciation and feedback for all the things that are done well or better than before.

With respect to curriculum, children need to be active in their studies. Basic skills are not the center or the end of learning, but the tools children need to use for acquiring content. It will help to focus plans in education on providing more substance by seeing basic skills *applied* to content areas: using measurement to find out more about the physical world and social world, using reading to build a model, and using writing to be in touch with somebody far away.

In all these endeavors, you are really not alone. As indicated earlier, teachers talked with one another, with a principal, with a psychologist, or with a parent. In the next chapter, beyond venting and blaming, we will consider how teachers can find support and help from other adults.

QUESTIONS TO CONSIDER

1. In which three activities in your classroom do your children seem to be most self-directed? Why do you think this is so?
2. In which three activities in your classroom do your children seem to be least self-directed? Why do you think this is so?
3. What three concepts do you enjoy teaching more than others? Why do you think this is so?
4. What three concepts do you enjoy teaching least? Why do you think this is so?
5. Using the guidelines presented in this chapter, how could you improve your teaching enjoyment level as you teach one of your least favorite concepts?
6. What steps can you take to build the social acceptability to other children of one of the less socially accepted children in your classroom?

BOOKS AND FILMS ON PHYSICAL DISABILITIES

Barnes, E., Berrigan, C., & Biklen, D. *What's the difference? Teaching positive attitudes toward people with disabilities.* Syracuse, N.Y.: Human Policy Press, 1978.

Benham, H. (Ed.) *Scholastic feeling free activities and stories.* New York: Scholastic Book Services, 1978.

Biklen, D., & Sokoloff, M. (Eds.). *What do you do when your wheelchair gets a flat tire?* New York: Scholastic Book Services, 1978.

Get it together. 20 minutes, color. Santa Monica, Calif.: Pyramid Films, 1976. (Film)

My son, Kevin. 24 minutes, color. Directed by Allan Segal, Granada International Television, 1974. Distributed by Wombat Productions, 77 Tarrytown Road, White Plains, N.Y. 10607. (Film)

Nicky: One of my best friends. 15 minutes, color. New York: McGraw-Hill, 1975. (Film)

Shaver, J., & Curtis, C. *Handicapism and equal opportunity: Teaching about the disabled in social studies.* Reston, Va.: The Foundation for Exceptional Children, 1981.

6

Working with Colleagues and Volunteers

When a child who has special learning needs becomes a member of your class for part or all of the day, you can find help by sharing ways of working with colleagues. Sometimes, teachers get together and share anecdotes of recorded child behavior in order to consider alternative ways to plan.

The section below, "Individual Education Plans," traces how several cases of children with special learning needs were problems for their teachers, even though there was a formal team-developed Individual Education Plan (IEP). What they needed was some help in translating the IEP into actions and activities that made sense in terms of their franchise to act as teachers.

When teachers literally "share" a child at different times during the day or week, it is terribly important for them to dovetail observations and to share ideas that work for them, for the other children in the group, and for the particular child. It helps when principals anticipate this need for teachers to communicate and schedule prep times or lunch periods at the same time. If this is not the case, make the suggestion to the principal that people who need to communicate should have overlapping schedules.

Another way for teachers to share, whether it be present and former teachers, present and future teachers, or present teachers from various departments, is to communicate what has worked best with a particular child. The section on feedback loops records some ways that other people have helped, in person by feedback and coaching, and with written communication.

Even an experienced teacher who is working with a different age group for the first time or with a child who has special learning needs will do better to have coaching or feedback in dealing with this new behavioral profile. Especially in working with children who have special learning needs, the big task for a teacher is to define the often irregular profile of behavior. For example, a child with special needs in some areas may be fully adequate in other areas. Learning to understand what the behavior means can help you to adapt your actions and activities to the children's needs.

Even with cooperative efforts among teachers and careful planning, occasional emergencies arise. One child may have a seizure; another child may explode with anger during the course of a school year. Suggestions for coping with these and other crises appear in a section on emergencies.

"Extra hands" for emergencies and for other program support are important resources for which you will need to plan. There are some effective ways that teachers have found to work well in integrating extra hands into their programs. These ways are discussed in the closing section of this chapter.

INDIVIDUAL EDUCATION PLANS

ALVIN, FOURTH GRADE

Alvin was described by Ms. Z., his fourth-grade teacher, as the "bane of her existence." "He's a bright boy, anyone can see that . . . but lazy. If he'd only try harder he could complete his work. His homework is a disgrace! It's sloppy, if it's turned in at all. Now that he's broken his leg, he's worse than ever. With the cast and crutches it takes him longer to get from place to place. He's been using the accident as an excuse for not completing any homework this past week."

It was clear to Dr. G., the school psychologist, that Ms. Z. could spend hours describing Alvin. Unfortunately most of what she'd said about Alvin, although negative, was true.

Alvin had come before the district's Committee on the Handicapped earlier that fall but was not found to be in need of special education services. Although his written work had been described as "messy and disorganized" by all his previous teachers, it seemed much more so when compared with the work of others in fourth grade. Psychological and academic testing revealed him to be a bright child who obtained on-grade or above-grade level scores in all the achievement areas. His writing was a weak point. Letters and words were poorly formed and spaced. Sentences were grammatically incorrect.

On the whole, Alvin's major difficulty lay in organizing the time and space in his life. He often underestimated the amount of time it would take to complete a task. According to his parents, Alvin's room at home was "a nightmare" and his homework routine "nonexistent." They indicated that nagging was the only technique that worked—if they didn't become too tired of hearing their own voices beforehand.

What Does "Needs Structure" Mean?

Depending on who reads the recommendation, this phrase can mean many different things. Typically it refers to a general need for more external organization in the school or home environment including physical structure. In some children the need for structure is so great that many classroom routines must be broken down into specific behaviors and rehearsed every day. In other children, more structure refers to a need for more explicit instructions and a greater use of models when giving assignments.

Figure 6.1 presents an excerpt from an Individual Education Program for Alvin, a youngster who needs more structure in school and at

---

Figure 6.1 Selected Portions of the Individual Education Program for Alvin, Grade 4

Name: Alvin   Grade 4

Summary of Present Level of Educational Performance:

Strengths	Areas in Need of Improvement
- Bright average intellectual functioning	- Organization skills, especially in written work

- Academic achievement:
  Reading: 6.5
  Math: 5.9
	- Handwriting

Name: Alvin

Annual Goal Priority # (1) Improvement of organizational skills in written work

Short Term Objectives:	Special Materials/Methods
Alvin will be able to complete short written assignments based on analogies at least 50% of the time assigned	- Teacher-developed synectics materials - Adapted individualized language arts program (Weehawken)

---

home. He needs yet another variation of structure, especially in his written work. His teacher decided to work on shorter writing assignments, writing assignments with built-in benchmarks, time constraints through the provision of a kitchen timer, the regular scheduling of computer time, and the development of a homework checklist.

Short writing assignments included such activities as stretching exercises at the recognition level using direct analogies drawn from Synectics (Gordon & Poze, 1972, 1973).

How is a venetian blind like a pair of curtains?
How is a venetian blind not like a pair of curtains?

How is a venetian blind like a hundred eyelids?
How is a venetian blind not like a hundred eyelids?

How is a _____ like _____? Why?
How is a _____ not like _____? Why?

Other items that can fit this model include the following:

paper clip: mousetrap
spider's web: mousetrap

The sentence pair is helpful in building stretch, or distance, between the referent and its analogue in direct analogies. Comparing a living with a nonliving thing builds greater stretch.

A longer type of writing assignment was developed by combining the use of personal analogy (Synectics) and linguistic writing techniques adapted from the Individualized Language Arts program (Weehawken, 1974; Rothstein, 1981; Rothstein & Gess, 1982). Benchmarks were built in by setting out a series of shorter, separate tasks as presented in figure 6.2.

Ms. Z. had these instructions typed on separate 5" × 8" index cards (smaller ones tended to be lost more easily) but only made one or two cards available to Alvin at a time. She gave Alvin feedback after cards 2, 3, 6, and 7. At the same time that Alvin had frequent feedback, he also had a sense of independence because teacher monitoring did not occur after each card. Together with Alvin, Ms. Z. worked out setting the kitchen timer for cards 1, 2, and 7.

The planning and writing activity took place at a table facing the wall in an uncluttered area where Alvin could stretch his leg and rest his crutches. To further assist Alvin, Ms. Z. set a small table lamp on the table, further setting off the area, and enhancing the atmosphere of concentration.

Ms. Z. could schedule time on a portable microcomputer several times each week for Alvin. Using "Legends" software in PILOT language (Apple, 1982), Alvin felt encouraged to concentrate and to perform more competently than usual.

Alvin's parents reported that the shared homework checklist shown in figure 6.3, photocopied on blue paper so that it was more easily found among the white looseleaf pages, was useful when reviewing Alvin's position that his homework was done.

In a similar fashion, Ms. Z. used Alvin's clipboard each day to hold a shared schedule for the day. As shown in figure 6.4, it contained two columns: class schedule and personal schedule. Ms. Z. had photocopied

---

Figure 6.2 Sample Breakdown of Writing Assignment

1. Personal Analogy. Imagine that you are a box of spaghetti (a teabag, a wheel on an eighteen-wheeler truck, a dishwasher). Become the thing.

2. Brainstorm. What might you see, hear, feel, look forward to, wish? List words that can save your experience for you.

3. Outline. Use short phrases.

    Opening: Where will you be? How will you be there?

    Middle: What will happen to you?

    What are your feelings?

    What are your wishes?

    What else will you do?

    Why will you take that action?

    Why do you feel as you do?

    Closing: What might happen to you?

    How do you feel about it?

    What can you look forward to?

4. Draft. Write full sentences in a first draft using the outline.

5. Exchange writing with a writing buddy in the conference area of the classroom.

6. Revise or share with the teacher.

7. Rewrite in notebook for saving.

Figure 6.3 Sample Homework Checklist

CATEGORIES	Days of Week																			
	Mon		Tues		Wed		Thurs		Fri		Mon		Tues		Wed		Thurs		Fri	
	yes	no	yes	no	yes	no	yes	no	yes	no	yes	no	yes	no	yes	no	yes	no	yes	no
1. Are you ready to start at 7:00?																				
2. Is your assignment written down?																				
3. Did you bring all materials home?																				
4. Is your work done on looseleaf paper?																				
5. Is the paper unfolded and neat?																				
6. Is the proper heading on the paper?																				
7. Is your penmanship neat?																				
8. Is your work done in ink?																				
9. Is the assignment complete?																				
10. Did you pack everything to return to school?																				
Number of points scored																				
Total points for the week																				

<u>Figure 6.4 Sample of Personalized Day's Schedule</u>

		Date: 1/15 Name: <u>Alvin</u>	
<u>Class Schedule</u>		<u>Personal Schedule</u>	<u>Check Off</u>
8:50 Group Time	T	Listen. Raise hand.	_____
9:15 Language Arts		Card 3, Opening	_____
		Middle	_____
		Closing	_____
	T	Show Ms. Z.	_____
		If time, read chapter in	_____
		<u>Blubber</u> (Blume, 1976)	
		or take grab bag activity	_____
	T	10:00 Reading Group	
10:20 Math/Science		Card 9. Short division problems	_____
		Share with math buddy	_____
	T	10:40 Math Group	_____
		11:00 Science Center	
		Gram weights problems	
		11:30 Record findings in notebook	_____
		Compare with math buddy	_____
11:40 Story	T	11:40 Listen	_____
12:00 Lunch			_____
12:45 Reading Independently			_____
1:10 Social Studies			
Planning Trip to			
Newspaper	T	Listen, Raise hand	_____
		Copy details in notebook	_____
1:40 Social Studies Activities		Reading Teacher (out of class)	_____
		2:10 Join diorama group	_____
2:40 Close down, cleanup		If time, continue checker game	_____
2:55 Home			

T = Teacher working with Alvin

the class schedule in outline form and added variations for individuals as they were needed.

Alvin's parents also mentioned to Ms. Z. that their comments to Alvin had become more encouraging and supportive after they had participated in a "positive parenting group" led by the school psychologist. They had found the Positive Parenting Checklist, presented in figure 6.5, to be a helpful guide in thinking about the way they had typically interacted with Alvin, especially around homework issues.

CASEY, FIFTH GRADE

Casey impresses you immediately as an eleven-year-old child who is wired for action. Assigned to a regular fifth-grade classroom for half the day and to a resource center for children with special learning problems for the other half, Casey is a child with several learning problems. He has been described as having average ability to learn, a short attention span, and a poor memory for material that has been presented orally.

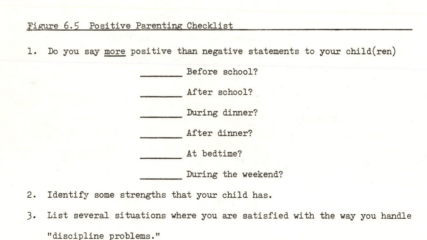

Figure 6.5 Positive Parenting Checklist

1. Do you say <u>more</u> positive than negative statements to your child(ren)

    _____ Before school?

    _____ After school?

    _____ During dinner?

    _____ After dinner?

    _____ At bedtime?

    _____ During the weekend?

2. Identify some strengths that your child has.

3. List several situations where you are satisfied with the way you handle "discipline problems."

4. List examples of your "reminding" statements. How are these different from nagging comments?

5. During the past year, how have your discipline strategies <u>reduced</u> the behaviors that disturbed you in the first place?

During the morning he can be found in the resource room working on reading and math activities that are approximately two-and-a-half years below his grade level. In this structured setting, his teacher works individually with him or in a small group that includes Casey and three other fourth or fifth graders. Short activities of ten to fifteen minutes are alternated with activities that require more time, fifteen to twenty-five minutes, as the children work with a variety of visual and concrete materials. Frequently, the teacher speaks to Casey in a low voice, telling him, "You've accomplished so much today" or "You're working very independently, Casey. Keep it up."

Although Casey works quickly, completing task after task in the resource room setting, his experiences in his regular classroom during the afternoon are very different.

An observer outside the door of Casey's fifth grade classroom might hear the following:

Mr. F.: Casey, come back to your desk this minute.
Casey: I can't do that work. Don't you know I have a learning disability?
Mr. F.: Learning problem or not, you have a social studies worksheet to complete.
Student: Mr. F., Casey took my pencil.
Casey: Take your old pencil, I'm leaving here anyway. (Casey walks toward the door.)
Mr. F.: You're not going down to the resource room again today, Casey. Try to act like a fifth grader instead of a first grader.

Mr. F. apparently is at the end of his patience with Casey. Not having him as a part of his class half the day, everyday, has made it difficult for Mr. F. to develop a close relationship with Casey. Casey's learning problems, which often result in his wandering around the room and disrupting other children, also make it hard for Mr. F. to feel positively about him.

What Does "Frequent Praise and Attention" Mean?

The answer to this question seems obvious. You praise children and give them attention when you see that they need it. The problem arises, however, when a child's need for positive feedback and teacher attention is greater than that of the rest of the class. This child may have developed effective ways of getting your attention more often than his or her peers but for the wrong reasons. You may be paying attention to calling out, wandering, or other distracting behavior and have little opportunity to praise at all.

Often a child who needs frequent praise and attention creates a cycle of inappropriate activity followed by negative teacher comment. Breaking this negative pattern is the major goal of a recommendation for frequent praise and attention. Figure 6.6 presents an excerpt from Casey's Individual Education Program, which calls for frequent praise and attention. Suggestions for implementing this recommendation follow.

Casey's teacher began by thinking in terms of Casey's feeling of being catapulted into a fifth-grade classroom during the afternoons when science, applied mathematics, social studies, and small-group projects were under way. After spending each morning in the resource room where the main menu was the 3Rs, Casey seemed to roam and occasionally disrupt. Mr. F. met this challenge by rethinking his afternoon goals and structure.

Mr. F. realized that Casey could not be expected to concentrate on social studies and science texts or writing assignments along with the rest of the class because his skills appeared to be two-and-a-half years below grade level. Yet, Mr. F. felt that the idea of a "short attention span" was usually not universal but relative to the tasks that he expected a child to perform. The teacher alternated shorter and longer activities for Casey that included some paper-and-pencil work and reading at a second-grade skill level. He also alternated concrete activities in which Casey was involved: (1) applying concrete materials to his own written work, and (2) being responsible to a small group of other students for periods of science experiments, social studies, or other projects. Mr. F. also placed Casey's work in the context of his own planning for subgroups and his own ongoing circulation in the classroom.

Concrete Materials.   Mr. F. found some arithmetic games that required simple addition and subtraction. Plastic discs for counting were nearby. The answer from each problem was matched to an alphabet code that spelled out the answer to a riddle. Building from one-word answers, Casey was able to complete the "riddled addition" exercise shown in figure 6.7 after seven different easier samples.

Social Responsibility and Concrete Materials.   In another applied arithmetic activity, Mr. F. paired Casey with a more able youngster to use a metric wheel for measuring the perimeter of a variety of school areas. For each area, they would record the dimensions. In turn, Casey's

Figure 6.6 Selected Portions of the Individual Education Program for Casey, Grade 5

Name: Casey   Grade 5

Summary of present level of educational performance:

Strengths	Areas in Need of Improvement
- Average range of intellectual functioning	- Academic Achievement:
- Works well with frequent praise and feedback	Reading: 2.5 grade level
	Math: 2.5 grade level
	- Short attention span to academic work; increase task completion
	- Poor social skills in large group situations
	- Poor memory for auditorially presented materials

Name: Casey

Annual Goal Priority # (1) Improve attention span to academic work and increase task completion

Short-Term Objectives:	Special Methods/Materials
Casey will be able to complete applied arithmetic tasks at the 2.5 level at least 50% of the time in his regular classroom.	- Teacher-made arithmetic games - Measuring wheel

Annual Goal Priority # (2) Improve Casey's social skills in the regular classroom (e.g., working cooperatively, getting along with peers and teacher)

Short term Objectives	Special Methods/Materials
Casey will be able to complete assigned social studies and science activities with one or more classmates at least 50% of the time.	- Teacher developed cooperative activities (e.g., measuring a variety of school areas) - Shaftel (1967) role-playing model - Use frequent teacher praise and attention

Figure 6.7 Riddled Addition

Why did Pac-Man cross the road?

$$
\begin{array}{ccc\ \ cc\ \ ccc\ \ ccccc\ \ cccc}
5 & 6 & 2 & 4 & 6 & 5 & 2 & 4 & 4 & 3 & 3 & 7 & 2 & 2 & 2 & 2 & 5 \\
+2 & +2 & +7 & +5 & +4 & +4 & +3 & +4 & +6 & +6 & +2 & +1 & +0 & +4 & +2 & +1 & +3
\end{array}
$$

Alphabet Code

18	1	0	3	8	11	7	5	4	14	13	15	16	12	10	17	20	2	6	9	21	19	23	26	20	25
A	B	C	D	E	F	G	H	I	J	K	L	M	N	O	P	Q	R	S	T	U	V	W	X	Y	Z

task would be to use the measuring wheel and then line up the addition problems with his partner. They would submit the problems to a "banking" group who would calculate the total perimeters. Casey and his partner would then rank order the totals in terms of the longest to shortest perimeters measured and set up a summary chart for the bulletin board.

The interface with a partner and another group provided Casey with ongoing attention, varied activity, and legitimate responsibility.

Several social studies projects that Mr. F. planned for Casey include the following:

Explorers' group. Casey read biographies of explorers written at his reading level as a basis for becoming part of a discussion group with others who also had read about explorers. The group pinned markers to a world map with key events noted.

Immigration museum. For this project, Casey helped the teacher and a group of four other children set up the display of memorabilia for a parents' lunch.

Oral history project. Casey's group planned questions to ask in interviews of senior citizens who lived near their school.

By integrating concrete materials and arranging for Casey to be needed by other children, Casey became increasingly focused in his work.

Planning Subgroups and Circulating.   Mr. F. found that it was easier to plan for his group of twenty-seven students during the afternoon period when he thought of them as six or seven groups of four or five members, respectively. Some groups were more structured and other groups less structured in their work. At the outset, Mr. F. planned the time and six or seven activities with the entire class. After everybody was settled in their groups, Mr. F. was able to circulate, pause to teach, and then to circulate again. As he circulated, he was able to appreciate children's accomplishments and to make a positive contact with Casey, in particular, every ten minutes or so.

Role playing social values was an activity in which the teacher participated directly with Casey and a group of seven other students, following the Shaftel model (Shaftel & Shaftel, 1967). This was an activity in which the students took part interdependently. Even so, Mr. F. had to remind himself to use positive functional language rather than evaluative language with Casey (for example, "You really thought about your statement. Good idea," rather than "good idea" alone). Mr. F. also tried to be near Casey when the group was making transitions from one activity to another. His presence was a support to Casey as well as a natural opportunity for positive contact at a potentially unfocused time.

JENNY, THIRD GRADE

Jenny is a third grader. Her hearing is fine, but she becomes confused easily when too much is said to her. She spends part of each day in the building's resource room where she works with a special education teacher and two other students who have similar difficulties. They concentrate on reading activities that stress visual clues and on strengthening their listening skills.

Mr. L., Jenny's teacher, recognizes that Jenny has unique learning needs. He comments frequently, however, that he has twenty other students who also need his attention. His reaction to the resource room teacher's suggestion that he reinforce the objectives on Jenny's Individualized Education Program was quick: "How am I supposed to follow these goals? I barely understand them . . . and I'm the only adult in this classroom with twenty-one children!"

Mr. L.'s concerns are common. A dedicated teacher, he wants to do what's best for his students, but he finds it difficult to translate the jargon on an Individual Educational Program into activities that are suitable for the larger groups of children in his classroom.

What Does "Learns Best with Concrete Materials" Mean?

You probably have raised this question several times already if you have worked with children who have difficulty with the typical school curriculum beyond first grade. Children whose language development is delayed or whose listening skills seem poor for their age or grade placement get lost easily in the highly verbal world of many elementary classrooms. These children need more visual aids and "hands on" activities if they are to succeed in school. Figure 6.8 presents an excerpt from the Individual Education Program for Jenny, a child who learns best with concrete materials. Suggestions for implementing this recommendation follow.

Jenny's teacher began by cataloging areas for planning and decided to work on (1) a writing approach to reading, and (2) adding concrete materials and activities to the arithmetic work. Since Jenny spent part of the day away in the resource room, Mr. L. was considering (3) the use of a regular small group assignment for Jenny in order to help integrate her socially.

Writing into Reading.   Mr. L. had developed several dozen writing folders, each of which contained vocabulary around a topic. For example, there were three-part folders of holiday-related words, seasonal words, electrical words, city words, community worker words, geography words, zoo words, circus words, supermarket words, and so forth. When open, each folder was set up as a triptych, forming a kind of study carrel, as shown in figure 6.9.

After a small-group discussion on a particular subject, Mr. L. made sure that Jenny had a vocabulary folder from which she could work in her own writing book. He provided her with cartoon and magazine pictures for which she would write captions. He also gave her pictures that provided many visual clues in order to help her read preprinted labels and captions.

Concrete Arithmetic.   Mr. L. planned both individual and partner tasks in arithmetic for Jenny. Individual tasks involved the use of Cuisenaire rods and a balance scale with objects. Task cards held both pictures and captions.

Cooperative Group Work.   Partnered activities involved doing interview surveys and measuring together. With her partner, Jenny needed to

Figure 6.8 Selected Portions of the Individual Education Program for Jenny, Grade 3

Name: Jenny   Grade 3

Summary of present level of educational performance:

Strengths	Areas in need of improvement
- Average range of intellectual functioning	- Academic achievement:
- Makes good use of visual cues	Reading: 2.0 grade level
- Good visual-motor coordination	Math: 1.5 grade level
- Good peer relations	- Poor auditory discrimination
- Learns best through concrete materials	and memory
	- Difficulty with auditory
	processing

Name: Jenny

Annual Goal Priority # (1) Improve math achievement in the basic operations of addition and subtraction

Short Term Objectives	Special Methods/Materials
Jenny will be able to identify equivalent lengths of materials up to 10.	Cuisenaire rods
Jenny will be able to demonstrate reversibility with concrete materials.	

Annual Goal Priority #2 Improve reading achievement to a level of independent reading

Short term objective	Special Methods/Materials
Jenny will be able to read and comprehend materials in the context of illustrated clues.	- task cards with cartoons and/or pictures. - commercial materials.

listen in order to record responses. Partners helped to self-check for accuracy. For example, partners would take turns either asking for or recording responses to such surveys as:

How many people live in your home?
Does your mother smoke? Does your grandmother smoke?
Which of these three television shows is your favorite?

Figure 6.9 Vocabulary Folder of Sound-Related Words

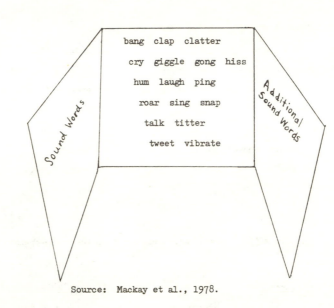

bang clap clatter

cry giggle gong hiss

hum laugh ping

roar sing snap

talk titter

tweet vibrate

Source: Mackay et al., 1978.

This procedure helped to provide practice in following auditory directions in a monitored way.

Mr. L. used "Stand Up" types of games in order to strengthen her listening skills in a concrete way and to help her become a more involved, albeit part-time, group member. "Stand Up" is from the *New Game* series (Fleuegelman, 1976) and involves one- and two-step directions in a cooperative vein, as follows: "Sit on the ground, back-to-back with your partner, knees bent and elbows linked. Now simply stand up together. With a bit of cooperation and a little practice, this shouldn't be too hard" (p. 65). The number of participants can include up to an entire class or more.

FEEDBACK LOOP: SPECIAL EDUCATION TEACHERS AND REGULAR TEACHERS

Visiting and Feedback: Integrating a Child with Special Learning Needs

While the preceding section mentioned how people with different roles in a school can learn to understand each others' language usage, there is an ongoing need for classroom teachers to communicate with others in the school who have additional information that can help a child's learning. The following section demonstrates a model for regular and special educators to share information on an ongoing basis.

SOMEBODY DO SOMETHING!: A CASE FOR BETTER COMMUNICATION

It appeared to be a routine request for assistance. Ms. D., the elementary level art teacher, said that she was having difficulty with her last period, sixth-grade art class. Ms. C., the principal, was surprised at this admission since Ms. D. had proven herself to be a very capable teacher throughout their six years of working together.

Ms. C.: What seems to be the trouble?

Ms. D.: Those three children from the special ed. program have got to go! They persist in disrupting the other children. They seldom complete any of our projects, and they're beginning to talk back to me.

Ms. C.: Would it help if I came tomorrow afternoon to observe? Perhaps together we can come up with a plan of action.

Ms. D.: All right, but I don't really know what you'll be able to do short of placing Lucy, Scot, and Joe back with their own special education teacher. Maybe I should teach them art in their own classrooms with the other special education children.

Ms. C.: Before we decide anything, let me visit you tomorrow.

Ms. C. entered the Art room at 1:40 the next afternoon. The children had been instructed to continue working on heart-shaped collages for Valentine's Day.

JOEY: Look out, Ms. D., he's got the scissors.

Ms. D.: Enough of that, Scot, give me the scissors if you can't cut out a simple heart like the other students. (Scot continued to brandish the scissors, skipping around the table where he had been assigned to work.)

LUCY: Ooh, ooh, Scot's going to cut someone!

Ms. D.: Lucy, go back to your table. That outline you made needs a lot of work.

All right, give the scissors here, Scot.

SCOT: Okay, okay, take your dumb old scissors. They're for babies anyway.

Ms. D.: Let's settle down, class. John, Barry, Sue, Stacy, you've done beautiful work today.

Lucy, Scot, Joey, continue on your collage work. Be careful not to overlap the various shapes too much. The contours are so interesting.

JOEY: (mumbling) What's she talking about anyway?
STACY: Sh., Sh. You're so dumb, Joey. You don't know anything. (Joey, grabbing Stacy's pile of magazine clippings, runs over to Scot's table.)
JOEY: Scot, look at these. I bet they can fly! (He drops the paper over Sue and Barry's work area.)
MS. D.: Enough, enough. Put away your work, class, and sit with your hands folded until it's time to return to your class. It's too bad that Ms. C. had to see our display of immaturity today.
JOEY: (mumbling) There she goes again . . . always talking big words.

Ms. C. met with Ms. D. after school that afternoon. After she had shared her written recordings and observations with Ms. D., Ms. D. commented that they looked like the script for a new situation comedy . . . except that she didn't feel like laughing.

MS. D.: I know that I let those three get to me, but I'm at the end of my patience. Why do they act that way?
MS. C.: I don't have a simple answer for you but I have a suggestion. Let's meet with Mr. M. and Ms. G. (the special education teachers) tomorrow at 11:00 and find out more about Lucy, Joey, and Scot. If I had known that you were having so much difficulty, we would have met as a group long before now.

The group of teachers and principal met as planned the next day. Within a short period of time, the art teacher discovered that Scot and Lucy had great difficulty with any activities that required eye-hand coordination. Clearly, using scissors efficiently or drawing various designs was going to present a problem for them. Mr. M. explained that Scot refused to consider that he had a problem in this area. He was much more likely to refuse to do tasks that were hard for him. "He'd much rather be a clown than admit to needing help" was his teacher's observation. "Lucy, on the other hand, manages to wander away from activities that she finds hard."

Ms. G. asked about Joey's behavior in listening and following directions during art. The art teacher commented that Joey did not complete most activities. "He's in his own world, I think. He doesn't ask me for help so I figure that he just doesn't like to stay with work too long."

Ms. G. then shared with Ms. D. additional background information about Joey's problems in understanding and following verbal directions. "When I show him what to do, give him models or samples, he'll do just fine. When I forget and just give a series of directions, he's in trouble. More often than not he'll start the activity and then begin to wander or stir up action in another part of the room."

Ms. G. and Mr. M. had brought along copies of the Individual Education Program that they had prepared for Joey, Scot, and Lucy. As Ms. D. read through them, she commented, "I wish I had seen these before. Maybe I could have made some changes in my plans so that I didn't bump into their problems with each new activity."

The special education class teachers agreed to make copies of the IEPs for the art teacher. Ms. D., however, mentioned that she was unfamiliar with the meaning of some of the test data and comments about specific learning disabilities. She asked for a summary instead, "in English," she laughingly suggested.

With a plan to continue meeting periodically to discuss the children's progress in art class, the special education teachers asked Ms. D. if she would share some of the activities that she planned to do with the children. "Perhaps we can work some of the vocabulary that you'll be using into our language arts lessons," offered Mr. M.

Ms. C., the principal, had remained in the background during most of the preceding meeting. Near its completion, however, she presented the group with an idea for facilitating communication between regular and special educators on a regular basis. She suggested that the special educators complete a brief checklist about each of their students who would be entering the mainstream. A copy of this checklist would be given to the art, music, gym, or regular classroom teacher *before* the children joined their groups. The elective area and regular classroom teachers, in turn, could share information about particular activities that they were planning with the special education teachers. Although neither group of teachers was excited about the prospect of having more paperwork, they agreed that the exchange of more information about the children's special learning needs would be a help to everyone in the long run.

Several meetings later a draft emerged of each form for sharing. See figure 6.10 for the checklist to be filled out by the special education teacher, and figure 6.11 for the form an elective area teacher would complete.

Idealized Scenario

The art teacher and the special education teachers were delighted with their recently developed communication system. With the beginning of a new marking period, and of new art projects to complete, they

Figure 6.10 Special Education/Special Subject Area Communication Form

To: (Special Area Teacher) _____ Re Student: _____

From: (Special Education Teacher) _____ Date: _____

  Reading level: _____ Age of Student: _____

  Math level: _____ Grade: _____

		Weak			Strong
Behaviors Related to Learning					
1.	Eye-hand coordination	1	2	3	4
2.	Ability to follow oral directions	1	2	3	4
3.	Ability to follow written directions	1	2	3	4
4.	Ability to participate in group discussion	1	2	3	4
5.	Memory for auditorially-presented information	1	2	3	4
6.	Memory for visually-presented information	1	2	3	4
7.	Ability to benefit from demonstration of desired behavior or procedures	1	2	3	4
8.	Ability to work independently	1	2	3	4
9.	Ability to tolerate working at a slower pace/lower level than peers	1	2	3	4
10.	Ability to work with a peer without disruptive behavior	1	2	3	4

	Likelihood of Success for Various Task Modifications	Poor			Good	Not Necessary
1.	Use of tape-recorder instead of written materials	1	2	3	4	
2.	Use of a "buddy system" to complete various tasks	1	2	3	4	
3.	Increasing teacher feedback for work completed or attention to task	1	2	3	4	
4.	Simplifying the presentation of directions:					
	1 step	1	2	3	4	
	2 steps	1	2	3	4	
	3 steps	1	2	3	4	

Additional Comments:

were eager to see the practical results of their information exchange. Ms. C., the principal, again offered to visit the sixth grade "mainstreamed" art class to observe any changes in procedures and children's behavior that may have resulted from the communication network. Ms. C. entered the art room at 1:40 on Wednesday afternoon. The children were involved in making travel posters.

Figure 6.11 Elective Area Information Sharing Form

NAME OF TEACHER: _____   DATE: _____

SUBJECT AREA: _____   Dates on Which Activity

Will Be Covered in Class _____

1. Description of specific activity:

2. Vocabulary (listening/written) necessary for completion of the activity:

3. Materials which will be used:

4. Skills which I expect the student to demonstrate during/after completion
   of the activity:

5. Prerequisite skills/concepts:

SCOT: Ms. D, what do you think of this? The picture of the White House here and the cherry trees along here?

Ms. D.: That's a great plan! You've combined the cut-out pictures and your own drawings beautifully. (A supply of precut pictures of well-known buildings, gardens, and other travel-related scenes had been prepared by a group of children prior to this project. These materials were available to anyone who wanted to include them in their posters. In addition, paints, markers, craypas, glue, scissors, and travel brochures were organized at each of the five round tables.)

Ms. D.: Joey, may I see your work plan again? We may need to add an extra step.

JOEY: Sure, Ms. D., but this "blueprint" is just like a professional now.

Ms. D.: O.K. Joey, where will you add the cardboard backing?

JOEY: O-o-o darn, I thought I did that! Well, maybe here? (He pointed to the space before the final box on a small flow chart placed to the right of his poster paper.)

Ms. D.: Excellent . . . you're becoming quite a planner!

LUCY: Ms. D., it's my turn now. Scot and Joey will be finished before me.

Ms. C. smiled at Lucy's comment. It was in sharp contrast to the whining complaints made about her classmates a month ago. There were several other changes in this setting compared to the previous visit.

Scot, who was described as having difficulty with fine motor coordination, especially in cutting and detailed drawing and writing activities, had a new option available to him. The supply of precut pictures enabled him to include detailed illustrations in his poster without the burden of cutting and/or sketching them himself. There was no stigma attached to this option since the precut selections were available to everyone.

Joey, who had acted-out instead of listening, an area of particular difficulty for him, now had a flow chart to guide his activity instead of seldom-heard teacher directions. With a visual plan of action in front of him, Joey was much more likely to succeed on a task and therefore to stay with it instead of wandering off.

PROBLEMS AND EMERGENCIES

It is really wonderful when you have time to plan ahead and have the luxury of collaborating with other adults. In the real world, though, emergencies arise when you feel as if you are the last living adult.

Tempers flare, seizures occur, and impulsive behavior can lead to danger. As several teachers have had such emergencies occur and, most importantly, have survived, it makes sense to share some of these experiences. To begin, imagine witnessing the following fight in a fifth grade classroom.

Fighting in the Classroom

"Take it back, Michael. Take it back."

"I will not. You jerk. You're always saying things to me."

"Now it's my turn. You're stupid. You're ugly."

"Think you're so big. Take that . . . and that."

With that, Leon and Michael, two larger-than-average fifth graders, began slugging one another in front of Ms. A.'s shocked students. Ms. A. called to them to stop, to act their age. Seeing quickly that her words were futile, she walked toward the other children. "Steve, go to the office and get Mr. D. fast. Tell him it's an emergency."

Michael and Leon had fallen to the floor within the several minutes that it took Steve and Mr. D. to return. Ms. A . cleared the other children away from the fight, toward the rear and side of the classroom. Ms. A. and Mr. D. separated the boys by pulling each apart from the rear. "Stop it now, Leon." "Cut it out, Michael. Enough." Ms. A. and Mr. D. stood between the two boys. The other children looked on in shock. Fighting was something that happened on the playground, not inside, not in front of teachers!

"If you'll stay with my class while I speak with these two outside, Mr. D., I'd appreciate it." Ms. A. remained between the two as they walked out of the classroom to the corridor. She faced them both and said firmly, "This is *not* acceptable behavior in our class. As soon as the rest of the class goes to gym, we will talk about consequences for this behavior."

With Mr. D. covering her class, Ms. A. stayed with Leon and Michael. In a few minutes her class left for gym when their physical education teacher appeared in the doorway.

Ms. A.: All right, now. One at a time. Tell me, Michael, what happened.

MICHAEL: Leon started . . . he . . .

Ms. A.: Wait, Michael. Back up. Tell me what you did. Begin with "I . . ."

With Ms. A. calmly looking at and listening to each boy in turn, Leon and Michael gradually told what they had done immediately before and during the recent skirmish. After they had concluded the "statement of facts" that described their *own* actions, in their *own* words, Ms. A. asked Michael, then Leon, "What did this do to help you? What did you gain from it?"

Although this verbal exchange seems lengthy, it lasted only several minutes. Ms. A.'s initial purpose had been accomplished: Encourage each of the boys to admit their own actions, rather than blame one another.

Ms. A.: What do you think should happen now, Michael? Leon? What is
the consequence for fighting in our classroom?

LEON: (mumbling) We gotta clean up the mess we made.

MICHAEL: Yeah, and do the whole room this afternoon . . . the rest of the
week, too.

Ms. A.: That's right, that's the rule we set up in September. Now that the
consequence is settled, can you two think of another way to handle
your differences?

MICHAEL: (grumbling) It doesn't matter. I still don't like to be called names.

Ms. A.: You get angry when he calls you names, Michael. Can you think of
any other ways to let Leon know how you feel?

MICHAEL: Well, you know, not let him see me get mad . . . just walk away.

Ms. A.: That's one way to handle it. Can you think of anything else?

MICHAEL: Maybe laugh in his face, maybe spend more time with Steve and
Todd and forget about him for a while.

Ms. A.: I think you're on the right track. Maybe you can show Leon that
you won't spend time with him when he's name calling. Leon, you
said you were mad at Michael for calling you stupid and ugly.

LEON: That's right. He can't get away with that. I can't help it if I'm not as
good in reading as he is.

Ms. A.: You were upset when Michael made fun of you by calling you stupid. How else could you have let him know that you felt badly?

LEON: I don't know. Just because I go to that dumb resource room people
think I'm stupid. Maybe I'll stop going there.

Ms. A.: You think that by staying away from the resource room the other
children will stop teasing? It's a possibility. Can you think of another
solution?

LEON: Maybe not let them bother me . . . you know, ignore them. Talk to
the other kids, like Steve and Paula, who go to the resource room
with me.

Ms. A.: That's a good idea, Leon. Pay more attention to your other friends
and the name callers will see that they can't get you angry.

Ms. A.: You two seem to have calmed down. After you straighten up the
desks and chairs, you may go to gym. I'll see you this afternoon to
begin the rest of the cleanup.

What Worked in This School Crisis?   First, Ms. A realized that she needed help to separate the two children and to cover her class while she discussed the fight with the two "culprits." Instead of trying to intervene herself and risk getting hurt and/or appearing to be unable to control the situation, she sent to the office for assistance.

Second, she motioned the other children away from the fight and removed the fighters as soon as possible from the classroom, both to minimize peer attention and to provide an opportunity for calming down.

Third, she wanted Leon and Michael to accept responsibility for their own actions and to describe the consequences previously determined for classroom fighting. In order to do this, Ms. A. needed a quiet spot and sufficient time for an immediate conference. Her questions to each child were direct: "What happened? What are the consequences? Could you have done anything differently?"

This step was made more manageable because the consequences for fighting (and other serious infractions) had been developed by the class in September. Ms. A. did not have to get involved in a debate about causation and punishment. All forms of fighting were unacceptable. Anyone involved in a fight would share the consequences of (1) straightening up anything disturbed by the fighting and (2) cleaning the entire room every day for a week.

Ms. A. may have been upset by her students' fighting but she was not overwhelmed. Preplanning with her class enabled her to make the best of this crisis situation. Since she did not become embroiled in a debate with Leon and Michael, she maintained control and modeled for them calm, concerned behavior.

Figure 6.12 summarizes one set of emergency steps to take in case of a fight.

Running Out of the Room Without Permission

"Jason, come back to your table this minute. It's time for your group to do math puzzles." "A losing battle," thought Mr. M. as he walked toward Jason, one of the older students in his intermediate special education classroom. "That child is a study in motion." Jason had joined his group by the time Mr. M. had approached the table, and he had begun to arrange the Cuisenaire rods to solve an addition problem.

But within five minutes Jason had left the classroom. By the time Mr. M. had noticed his disappearance, Jason had roamed down one, then another corridor into the kindergarten wing. Alternately, he walked bent over with his arms swinging back and forth and jumping up so as

Figure 6.12 Emergency Steps in the Case of a Classroom Fight

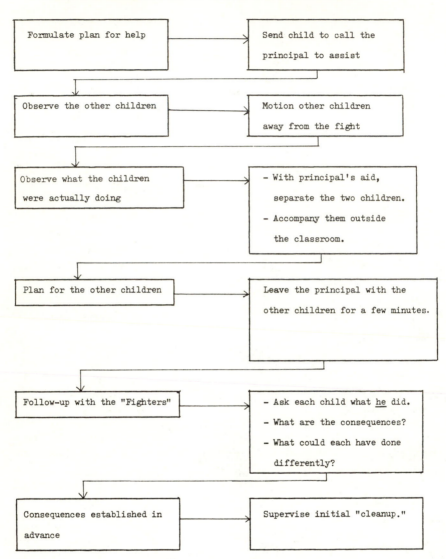

Formulate plan for help	Send child to call the principal to assist
Observe the other children	Motion other children away from the fight
Observe what the children were actually doing	- With principal's aid, separate the two children. - Accompany them outside the classroom.
Plan for the other children	Leave the principal with the other children for a few minutes.
Follow-up with the "Fighters"	- Ask each child what he did. - What are the consequences? - What could each have done differently?
Consequences established in advance	Supervise initial "cleanup."

to look into the windows of various classrooms. Jason had arrived at the rear entrance.

At that moment, Ms. McP. happened to open her door, which was next to the exit. Calmly, so as not to trigger a quick escape by the school's "Houdini," she commented, "Why, Jason, just the person to help us out. One of our guinea pigs has decided to play hide and seek. Would you help us look for her?"

Ms. McP. realized that she was taking the chance of rewarding his wandering behavior with her request to help but she remembered the incident that had occurred last month when Jason had disappeared in the neighborhood for two hours. He was within easy reach of another outdoor adventure, with one hand on the door handle and his foot against the door.

Ms. McP. had two choices if Jason chose to run: Leave her own kindergartners and run after him or remain inside, call for assistance, and let him get a head start. She decided on a diversionary tactic. If she could encourage him to join her students, she might prevent the escape altogether. She said, "Come in as soon as you are ready."

Fortunately, Ms. McP.'s hunch succeeded. In a few seconds, Jason strolled in looking sure of himself, and asked if he could hold the guinea pig when they found it. She assured him that he could but that they'd better hurry up. Before the hunt began, Ms. McP. called the office to tell them that Jason was assisting her class. After they had found and held Coriander, the guinea pig, Ms. McP. suggested that Jason return to Mr. M.'s classroom as he accompanied her group on their way to the auditorium.

What Worked in This School Crisis? Ms. McP., an unsuspecting bystander in Houdini's attempt, had little time to think before acting. In those few seconds, however, she made an important decision. Her first reaction, to speak calmly and enlist Jason's aid, instead of reprimanding him, was critical.

Briefly, Ms. McP. had reviewed her options: either running after Jason or standing by while he ran away. She prevented Jason from feeling cornered, and possibly pressured into running if he felt chased, by using a diversionary tactic.

With Jason engaged productively in her class's search for an errant guinea pig, Ms. McP. was able to praise him for his assistance. She maintained a matter-of-fact attitude regarding his presence in her classroom and his return to Mr. M.'s room by her casual phone call to the main office and her suggestion that he go back to his room while accompanying her class to the auditorium. Figure 6.13 summarizes the steps Ms. McP. took in dealing with this runaway child.

A Seizure Can Happen Anywhere

It was happening before Mr. C.'s eyes: Joey had fallen to the floor, stiffened, and had begun to move uncontrollably. His whole body con-

Figure 6.13 Emergency Steps in the Case of a Runaway Child

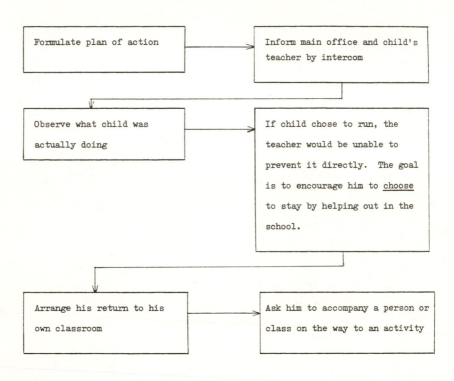

vulsed, his eyes rolled back, and saliva trickled on his chin. The children nearby looked shocked. Libby, Amy, and Caroline drew together whimpering, "What's wrong with Joey, Mr. C.? Is he going to die?" Chad and Jimmy pushed their chairs out of the way of Joey's feet.

"Good job, boys. Let's move the other chair away from Joey's head so that he doesn't bump himself," suggested Mr. C. After the initial shock of seeing Joey slide off his chair onto the floor and begin to shake spasmodically, Mr. C. was able to mobilize himself—and the other students. Although he knew that Joey had epilepsy, he had never witnessed a grand mal seizure. He recited his plan of action to the students, as much for his benefit as for theirs.

"Okay, we've moved any objects that could hurt Joey while his arms and legs are shaking. Let me unbutton his top button and turn him on his side. This way, if he vomits, he will not cough or choke." "Meg, please tell Ms. G., the nurse, that Joey is having a seizure. She'll call his parents." "Amy, will you finish gathering up your group's reading books. I'll explain to you and the others more about Joey's seizure later. He'll be fine in a few minutes. He's not in pain, but he can't control his body just now. John, you, Jenni, and the other children scheduled for band practice can pack up your instruments. I'll stay by Joey, until the seizure is over."

To the uninitiated, perhaps no other classroom emergency is anticipated with the same dread that an epileptic seizure produces. Many myths and misconceptions are associated with epilepsy. Since seizures occur rarely in most regular education settings, school personnel and students seldom have the opportunity to see what a seizure looks like or to discuss what one should do if it occurs during the school day.

The school nurse had told Mr. C. about Joey's seizure disorder, which is the more general term for a variety of behaviors that result from "a sudden discharge of electrical energy in the brain" (Gadow, 1979, p. 33). In Joey's situation, as with most people who have seizure disorders, medication can control all or most of the seizures.

Joey recently had gained several pounds and grown two inches. A growth spurt sometimes results in the current daily dosage of medicine not being strong enough to control the seizures as it had before. Revised doses and/or changes in medication usually bring the seizures under control again.

Mr. C. had asked Ms. G., the school nurse, about Joey's medication and possible side effects when she first discussed his seizure disorder. "He may act tired and sometimes act more irritable than usual. Otherwise, he's fortunate not to have problems with side effects."

Mr. C. had been concerned about the likelihood of a seizure occurring during his year with Joey. The nurse told Mr. C. that it was unlikely, but possible. "Joey has had only one seizure in school these past four years in our building and he's had only four in all during this time."

Mr. C. had many questions for Ms. G. that afternoon in September when she mentioned Joey to him. He was relieved to hear that Joey's seizure, if it were to occur in his classroom, would likely last from three to five minutes, based on previous experiences.

Although Mr. C. had hesitated to share his apprehensions about working with a child who had epilepsy with Ms. G., he used his meeting with her to develop a plan of action in case a seizure should occur in his classroom. Six months later, when Joey fell to the floor, Mr. C. put that plan into effect.

What Worked in This Classroom Crisis?   First, Mr. C. had gathered information about Joey's seizure disorder *before* there was a problem in his classroom. He had asked questions of the school nurse even though he was uncomfortable about sharing his anxieties with her.

Secondly, he had developed an action plan that was simple enough for him to memorize in case he was confronted with a seizure during the class day.

Third, he was able to remain calm enough to observe both Joey and then other children in order to determine his immediate next steps. His major concerns were the possibility of Joey hurting himself and the impact of the seizure on the other children. He wanted to maintain as normal a classroom atmosphere as possible.

Figure 16.14 summarizes one set of emergency steps to take in case of a seizure.

Child on a Rampage

It had begun like any other day in Ms. H.'s primary, self-contained, special education class. The twelve children, labelled as mildly mentally retarded and/or emotionally disturbed, had returned from lunch and were working individually or in small groups. Suddenly Brenda hurled her paint brush at Joey, tripped over the easel, and screamed, "I hate this . . . no good, no good." Throwing handfuls of papers on the floor, she repeated, "I hate this, I hate this." Ms. H. stuck her head out of the door to look for assistance. Seeing no one, she sent Ms. E., her assistant teacher, to the office for help.

The other children acted scared at first. Several ducked down to the floor, covering their heads. Others jumped about and began squealing, "Look at Brenda. She wild! She crazy!" Johnny and Paul laughed at Brenda's antics. Brenda looked at the children who were laughing and pointing at her and seemed to become even more energized by their reactions. She threw several puzzles and containers of "attribute" blocks onto the floor, looked at her audience, and headed for Ms. H.'s desk.

At this point Ms. H. felt that she had two options: stop Brenda by going after her and physically restraining her or remove the audience by engaging them in another activity until help arrived. Seeing that Brenda was not hurting herself or other children and that she seemed to be playing more and more to her classmates, Ms. H. decided to attend to the other children first. She was concerned that they would become even more frightened or agitated by a struggle to stop Brenda.

Thankful for the horseshoe game that had been set up along the rear wall during the indoor recess, Ms. H. quickly appointed Paul, who had been laughing, and Julie, who had shouted to Brenda, as captains. While asking Paul and Julie to be captains might be interpreted as a reward, the teacher weighed this possibility against the need to distract the group from Brenda and to engage their attention in a positive way.

Figure 6.14 Emergency Steps in the Case of a Seizure

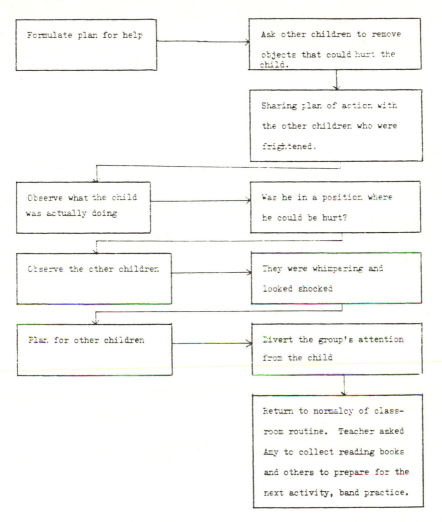

Ms. H. shrugged and told herself that after all, life can be a series of trade-offs. As first one, then the other child tossed their horseshoes, Ms. H. encouraged them with frequent comments, "That's terrific aim, how well you stand. Johnny, you're next. Sue, you wait so well."

Her rate of positive comments was much higher than usual since she was trying singlehandedly to pull the children's attention away from Brenda's performance to the seemingly more mundane game of horseshoes. As the game progressed, however, the children became more in-volved with it, helped no doubt by the tremendous amount of teacher and classmate praise and recognition.

Five minutes, that seemed like hours, passed before the assistant teacher, principal, and school social worker arrived. Brenda was still muttering and storming about the front of the classroom but she had lost a good deal of the momentum that had developed previously when the other children had "cheered her on."

What Worked in This Classroom Crisis? First, Ms. H. remained calm enough to formulate two plans: (1) send the assistant teacher for help, and (2) decide whether to restrain Brenda or to engage the other children's attention elsewhere.

Second, she observed what Brenda was actually *doing*: Was she hurting herself or other children? Was she causing permanent damage to school furniture or walls? Having answered "no" to these questions, Ms. H. realized that she could allow the rampage to continue a few minutes without serious harm.

Third, what were the other children doing? When Ms. H. saw that their behavior seemed to form a cheering section for Brenda she decided to intervene by diverting their attention, which was a powerful incentive for Brenda, from the rampage to a more productive, yet fun activity, like horseshoes. Finally, by encouraging the horseshoe players so visibly, so vocally, so often, she demonstrated that appropriate behavior is re-warded in her classroom.

Figure 6.15 summarizes what steps were taken in this emergency situation.

EXTRA HANDS: PARENTS, VOLUNTEERS, PARAPROFESSIONALS, AND PEERS

Mixed blessings may appear in a variety of forms, one of which is extra hands. At one time or another every teacher wishes for an extra pair of hands in the classroom. Trying to match activities to different chil-dren's learning styles, helping to manage different activities going on at the same time, and finding the just-right material on-the-spot are all occasions that benefit from additional helpers.

Using Helpers Effectively

As much as teachers may desire this association, many of us feel uncomfortable with other adults in the classroom. When you are fortu-

Figure 6.15 **Emergency Steps in the Case of a Rampage**

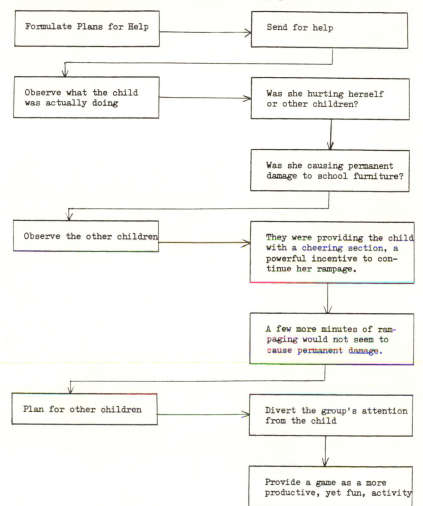

nate enough to find a naturally compatible assistant or volunteer with whom to work, or you see two adults working together harmoniously, it is possible to take for granted that extra hands can only help. However, be aware that they can also result in confusion, tension, and frustration that may be avoided if you plan ahead.

Adults may feel that they are tripping over one another in one situation or duplicating efforts in another. The helpers, too, may be frustrated if their desire to assist children in learning activities is eclipsed when they are relegated to folder stuffing or clerical tasks.

When two people work with children together, it is important for them to be clear, before the children arrive, just how they will share the responsibilities. For example, if there is an active science experience in the science area, and you had planned to teach a new concept to a group of eight children, then it would make sense that the assistant teacher or volunteer should plan to circulate among the other children who are participating in other preplanned activities. This may sound like simple common sense. However, it is surprising how often an assistant seems to be focusing attention on a youngster rather near the teacher while other youngsters at a distance may have a greater need for attention at that moment.

In order to make the best use of volunteers, teacher assistants, and peer tutors, the following questions need to be answered by the teacher *before* help arrives!

Questions	*Factors to Consider*
Who are the helpers?	Experience, educational background, goals? Adult/child peer?
What will they do?	Conceptual, social, or physical assistance? Academic or management tasks? Supplemental activities or direct instruction?
Where will they work?	Assigned locations or circulating among children, learning centers, or at children's seats?
When will they come?	Daily, weekly, monthly, mornings, afternoons, or parts? Regularly or sporadically?
With whom will they work?	Regularly assigned students or on an "as needed" approach? Whole-group/small-group/individuals?

While the teacher will answer these questions ahead of time, periodic cooperative planning with the assistant is likely to result in a greater degree of cooperation and participation among helpers.

Who Are the Helpers? In many special education classrooms a paraprofessional or teacher assistant is present for all or part of each day throughout the school year. The educational background of this person may vary from high school graduation to postcollege. Regardless of the educational background of the helper, it is important to recognize that the teacher is responsible for overall planning, management, and the delegation of activities for this assistant. The possible functions of this helper can vary from developing language experience stories with children to assisting with self-help skills (for example, zipping, buttoning, eating).

Although the scope of activities will vary dependent upon the capabilities of the helper, these activities will provide supplemental, rather than direct instructional, experiences.

In addition to teaching assistants employed by the school district, "extra hands" may belong to volunteers. These helpers may be parents of children in the class, grandparents, members of local senior citizens groups, or other adults from the community.

A third pool of potential helpers are children themselves, whether from an upper grade, another grade, or peers within the classroom.

What Will They Do? The actual learning experiences enhanced by your "helpers" will vary greatly dependent upon the skills of the person, the tasks of a particular lesson, and the age/developmental level of your students. Among the activities that teacher's assistants or volunteers have completed successfully are language experience stories, cooking activities, teaching the rudiments of a foreign language, making puppets for "language development theater," teaching their own unique skill (writer, folk singer), and supervising an activity area as a resource for materials.

For example, language experience stories call for the assistant to write down a child's words verbatim, as she or he dictates a story. Grammar is not of primary importance in this activity. The child learns that what is spoken can be written down and later read back by another person. The helper encourages the children to talk, to express their feelings without "pushing" them to say more than they want to say at that time. Effort is praised, regardless of the number of words, their arrangement, or their content. The helper functions as a supportive scribe.

As the teacher, you might list and then tell your helper what you expect and how it needs to be done for the benefit of the children. There is no reason to assume than an assistant will know how to do an activity if he has not worked with you before. It is always better to describe what you would like your assistant to do rather than to ask if he has done the activity before. Even if your assistant has worked with other teachers before, he may have done things quite differently than you expect in your classroom.

A peer might be involved in reviewing math facts, completing a social studies role-playing script, or assisting in feeding a needed word during free-reading time. A volunteer from the community, perhaps one of your children's parents, may be skilled in developing art and media displays. This parent can design, in consultation with your fifth graders, a bulletin board that highlights your latest creative writing activities.

An example of how an assistant could help in whole-group management would be in a self-concept lesson with six-year-olds. As the whole group of children sit on the floor, one target child sits on the teacher's lap. Children from the group take turns saying something nice about the target child (Donna Barnes, personal communication, 1979).

The assistant can help by moving unobtrusively along the edges of the group as needed and encouraging individual children to pay attention by whispering discreetly, "Let's hear what the next person is going to say," or by touching a child lightly on the arm, making eye contact, and pointing toward the speaker, indicating the need to listen. Similar assistance could be offered in any whole-group lesson.

Where Will They Work?   The assistant who roams around the edges of a whole-group activity would clearly be in the general vicinity of the teacher. Occasionally, a volunteer could work with an individual outside the classroom if greater concentration is needed and the classroom could serve as a distraction.

When in the classroom, it is important that, short of an emergency, the assistant work within a clearly defined territory. Otherwise this person will be available elsewhere only if there is an emergency. In this way, you can depend upon the relief of not having to supervise the defined territory.

When Will They Come?   Teachers always want to know when a helper will be there in order to be able to count on him. You need to have a regular schedule or to know a specific time and duration for a single event. You need to devise a method for the volunteer to let you know if he will be delayed or will not be able to come. If you have any doubt, consider an alternate plan for that particular time and group.

With Whom Will They Work?   Unless a volunteer or assistant comes with special skills, it is likely to expect that he will work with an individual or a small group of children. In one special education class, the assistant was assigned to three children who had difficulty following directions. After the teacher had introduced an activity, the assistant moved quietly from one of "her" children to another, providing additional information for one, redirecting another, and encouraging the third to complete the first step.

Although the assistant is assigned to a particular space and child or children, as the teacher you need to circulate, even if less often. The need for your skill in recognizing the precise moment for a fleeting teaching activity or the need to replan with the assistant is continuous.

Parent-Teacher Conferences: An Unexpected Source of Extra Hands

Parent-teacher conferences occur regularly in most schools. Who comes to these conferences? Very often they are the parents of children who are cooperative, who are doing well. In the faculty lounge, however, teachers comment on the children of those parents who do *not* appear at the twice-yearly meetings.

> "What do you expect? No wonder he's so disrespectful. His poor attitude probably starts at home."
> "If I could only see Howard's parents. The ones you want to come in never show!"

Imagine for a moment that Mr. G.'s "prize parents," Howard's father and mother, arrive at the next conference. Following his first impulse Mr. G.'s conference might begin this way:

> MR. G.: I'm really glad to see you. Howard is having a hard time this year. He doesn't pay attention during class and he doesn't do his work. He hasn't turned in any homework. I'd like you to talk to him about these things . . . let him know that you're concerned. Do you have any questions?
> FATHER: I get after Howard at home, too. He's very sloppy. Doesn't do much good, though.
> MOTHER: He does help sometimes . . . after I nag him. He just doesn't have any motivation.
> MR. G.: Well, I'd appreciate your speaking to him about his school work.

What happened during this exchange? Parents who had not been involved in their child's school experience very much previously, arrived at school. Their son's teacher greeted them with a barrage of negative information about Howard. He then requested vague assistance from home with nothing specific about *his* plans for Howard in the classroom. His comments about Howard's misbehavior triggered the parents to vent their own frustrations about their son.

The likelihood of positive growth in Howard is slight. Reviewing his parents' comments, we see that they already "talk to Howard" about various behaviors—and find this tactic to be ineffective. The burden of Howard's classroom difficulties has been dumped in their lap. In view of this less-than-rewarding experience, these parents may feel that they have been justified in avoiding school contact in the past.

What might have made this conference more successful for the parents, the teacher, and ultimately for the child? The major considera- tion should be given to preplanning on Mr. G.'s part. Although he may have wanted to share his frustrations with Howard's parents, he also wanted to enlist their cooperation in changing the child's behavior. By beginning with and highlighting negative behaviors, he has alienated parents who were not enthusiastic in the first place.

Planning ahead, thinking through the goal of this, or any, meeting with parents of your children may result in an extra pair of hands *at home* to assist in more positive classroom behaviors. Figure 6.16 presents a series of guidelines for conducting successful parent-teacher conferences. Additional valuable suggestions can be found in Kroth (1975) and Kroth and Simpson (1977).

SUMMARY

Cooperation and communication were the central issues to which this chapter was devoted. Whether discussing Individual Education Plans, mainstreaming, emergencies, or including extra helping hands in a class- room, schools need to provide opportunities for concerned adults to communicate about children and to cooperate in helping one another improve the experiences that children have in school.

When Individual Education Plans, developed by people from differ- ent backgrounds, summarize the need for a child to have "more struc- ture," or "frequent praise and attention," or "concrete materials," teachers need to translate these umbrella statements into nourishing drops of activities for each child.

A child who "needs more structure" might benefit from a personal schedule of activities with prearranged checking-in points and from directions that are broken into components with an example presented for each part.

Providing "frequent praise and teacher attention" follows naturally

Figure 6.16 Guidelines for a Successful Parent-Teacher Conference

PLAN Ahead

What are your goals?

- Developing and getting approval for an Individual Education Program?

- Problem Solving?

- Sharing test results?

- Asking questions that you want answered?

- Providing information you want to share? Emphasize the positive. Be specific and describe behavior.

- Describing your "next steps" in the classroom?

- Making suggestions for use at home?

BEGIN with a POSITIVE Statement

- "Howard has a great sense of humor."
- "He really enjoys materials that deal with animals."
- "He's sympathetic when somebody has a problem."

LISTEN actively. Empathize with the parents. Accept their feelings (e.g., "You seem to feel frustrated when Howard doesn't listen ").

Establish a PARTNERSHIP (e.g., "If you can ask to see his blue homework checklist sheet and ask him to review it at home, I can review it and chart his progress at school ").

Plan FOLLOW-UP CONTACTS. Notes or phone calls to share successes; keep parents informed before problems may develop.

END with a POSITIVE Statement

- "Howard has made several friends this year."
- "Howard should be a big help in the social studies play that a group is developing."

---

when you vary the length and type of learning activities and use positive language to comment on children's efforts as well as actual accomplishments.

To say that a child "learns best with concrete materials" means that the teacher needs to brainstorm alternatives to paper-and-pencil tasks.

When a child visits between two classrooms for "regular" and "special work," or becomes a member of one or the other kind of classroom, he or she is likely to have a better chance for success if the "sending" teacher shares with the "receiving" teacher those activities with which the child is likely to be successful. Also, it helps the child and teacher when a "sending" teacher shares with a "receiving" teacher those teacher behaviors that are most effective in making the child ready to learn and be comfortable in the setting. While personal communication is preferable, a minimal written communication checklist was presented for use in these situations.

Four classroom emergencies were discussed. These emergencies were drawn from the commonalities of crises offered by over a hundred practicing teachers in special education and regular elementary school settings. For each of these emergencies a set of guidelines was developed to help the teacher to cope. The following outline sketches common "emergency steps":

- Formulate plans for help
    Send assistant teacher or another child for help.
- Observe the target child(ren)'s actual behavior
    Is the child hurting him/herself or other children?
    Is the child causing permanent damage to school furniture or walls?
- Observe the other children
    What are they doing to add to or minimize the crisis?
- Plan for the other children
    Can you engage them elsewhere?
    Do they need to be reassured?
- Interact with the target child(ren) as necessary

Perhaps the most difficult step to take in an emergency is to *pause*, to think through alternatives, and then to react.

The concluding section dealing with integrating assistants, volunteers, peers, and parents in the classroom discussed some real problems in coordinating and communicating in order to provide a sincere and worthwhile education for children in school.

CONCLUSIONS AND REFLECTIONS

Collaboration takes time and, as anybody who has to think about budgets will agree, time is money. In the case of trying to place a price on helping children become more responsible and competent, the well-spent penny for prevention may save many dollars in remediation. (And, as noted earlier, simple scheduling of teacher preparation periods and lunch periods in common can fuel collaborative efforts at no additional cost.)

In any classroom, there will be children with diverse learning and management needs. When adults, regular educators, special educators, administrators, and support staff spend the shorter preventive time planning cooperatively and sharing information and insights about children, these diverse learning needs can be more nearly fulfilled.

However, sharing, cooperating, and communicating are processes that convey quite different content and products. We need to be sure that what is shared about children has a positive thrust. More often than we care to notice, frustrated adults will take a blaming attitude toward a child rather than to consider asking the questions: How can I organize differently? How might a different activity or a more concrete representation engage this child? How might I need to revise my expectations about this child's capabilities?

As a professional educator, each of us has a responsibility to influence colleagues in the best interests of children. When we talk or write about a child with others, let us try to use positive language and focus on a child's accomplishments, however small, in positive language.

QUESTIONS TO CONSIDER

1. What are the four or five emergency situations that you dread most as possible happenings during your teaching day? List several possible solutions. Refer to "Emergency Steps."
2. Select a child in your class about whom you feel uninformed. Look at the special/regular feedback loop. For what questions are you missing answers? Who can help you find some answers?
3. Who is the child in your class who caused you the greatest behavioral problem this year? What were a few moments when you felt successful in working with this child? Jot some notes to the teacher next year that point to what worked with this child.
4. Move down your class roster. Imagine you are preparing for a parent conference.
   a. What is one positive thing you can say about each child?
   b. What is one activity in which each child engaged?
   c. For which children do you need more information?

7

Teaching to Achieve
Your Goals

In this book, we have attempted to demonstrate an approach to classroom management, based on an analysis of behavior and curriculum, that you can apply in your learning environment. However, we have offered no sure-cure pills or instant remedies. Research concerning classroom organization and management indicates that there is a broad range of effective ways in which teachers practice. Whatever we do as teachers ultimately reflects our attitudes toward children.

We have proposed a way to plan for and establish a classroom structure and systems for working with children of varied abilities. This approach reflects positive teacher behavior that builds on children's successes and shows respect and enjoyment of children's capacities, regardless of age norms. It seems to us that positive teacher behavior that builds on children's successes is a key ingredient.

A sense of humor is also important. It is interesting to note that many teachers who have a sense of humor and appear to be comfortable and successful in working with children who have varied learning styles and needs use many of the ways of working that we have described without necessarily labeling them as such.

START-UP, CLOSE-DOWN: THE FIRST AND FINAL DAYS

Many teachers may say, "That sounds just fine if things (children, resources, principal, parents) were different. I don't have time to do that (work with subgroups, use inductive methods, employ concrete materials, engage in cooperative student learning activities, and so on). I have to *follow* the curriculum!" They make it sound as if we have an either-or situation: we must be either a spontaneous teacher who adapts plans creatively to stimulate children's understandings and critical possibilities, or a no-nonsense joyless teacher who focuses on isolated basic skills,

usually number facts and reading, so that children can do well on standardized tests.

First Days

It is possible to help children become responsible, independent, and
successful learners when the teacher plans ahead and begins to establish a
pattern of interaction from the first days of school. Perhaps the single
most important expectation that the teacher might establish during the
first days of school is that he or she is an appreciator—of efforts, personal
accomplishments, positive social contacts, responsible behavior, and so
on.

Among your primary tasks during the first days and weeks of school
will be helping children become increasingly self-directed and independent. Another important task will be to become familiar with each child's
capacities to work independently, to work with other children, and to
cope with the conceptual demands of various situations and materials.

In order to develop basic organizational patterns, it will be helpful
for you to plan to spend most of your energies circulating, particularly
showing your pleasure in the children's accomplishments.

You will need to watch and reinforce supportive traffic patterns,
observe attention spans in relation to different activities, notice social
needs, and consistently follow through with practical procedures for the
use and storage of materials.

While you may not expect to accomplish a major instructional program or breakthrough in the first few weeks if that would keep you from
circulating regularly for long periods of time, you may expect to do a
good deal of direct instruction and "fleeting teaching."

In addition, it makes good sense to review what children already
know and to diagnose needed next steps for instruction.

To plan for ways to develop responsible social behavior and to
minimize antisocial actions, it is useful to develop with children a set of
guidelines for working together and consequences to apply when the
system breaks down. Among human groups it is reasonable to expect that
rough times will happen. These same considerations can be used by
teachers of children in elementary school whether or not they have
special learning needs.

Final Days

While the first days of school establish the pattern and reflect what
you value about human nature, the final days of school can be an opportunity to reflect on what worked and what did not work so that you can

share these insights with the teacher next year. If you began the year as a new teacher concerned that you will not have enough ideas for things to do in the course of the year, that you might run out of ideas for activities, you will probably find that as the year draws to a close the opposite is true. There probably has not been enough time to do all the things that you would have liked to.

When you reflect back to the beginning of the school year, it is likely that you will appreciate the need to start the next school year with a consistent strong foundation of ways in which you and a new group of children can work together in satisfying ways. In retrospect, you can appreciate that you have built a stock of alternative activities and ways of working.

As you plan for closing down during the final days of school, it can be helpful to consider some of the following:

- Review objectives for different children and for the group as a whole (e.g., additional concrete activities in mathematics for an individual, a science fair)
- Plan for events that need completion (e.g., already begun multicultural or art projects)
- Set final program priorities with children as relevant (e.g., finish specific poetry readings)
- Translate these priorities into manageable activities (e.g., break down tasks according to daily or weekly time intervals)
- Set a time line—a plan of things to do and a schedule for doing them—for the final four to six weeks (see sample in figure 7.1)
- Share responsibilities with children and other adults as relevant

You may find that there is a natural resistance to letting go of relationships. Sometimes, this reluctance to face closing down tends to show in the human tendency to sprout new things to do, new directions to follow. If you feel this happening, consider where you need to focus your priorities and to what extent your time line has been realistic or can help to keep you involved in the tasks of completion and closing down.

When you share with children the tasks of close-down, it can help to leave you with a more satisfied feeling of completion rather than a sense of unfinished business and partings that have not been adequately expressed. For example, a positive future outlook for your group might be creating a summer address directory so that people can keep in touch.

If you have engaged in lots of small-group instruction, broken down tasks, and adapted them to different children, you may have observed that children have had similar experiences while engaging in different activities. We wish you the pleasure of taking a simple experience and

```
Figure 7.1  Closeout Time Line Sample

Task:     Science Fair

Week 1:   Analyze and chart findings (names)

Week 2:   Write up findings (names)
          Plan displays (names)
          Send invitations to fair (names)

Week 3:   Edit materials (names)
          Begin to execute display (names)

Week 4:   Finish displays (names)

Week 5:   Set up displays (names)
          Attend fair (whole class)

Week 6:   Dismantle fair (names)
          Evaluate fair (whole class)
```

seeing it expand as you "milk" a situation in fresh, unanticipated ways. You are likely to have more of these experiences of variety if you see your primary role as helping children to *use* their knowledge and skills rather than just to gain information and to acquire skills.

THE WEDDING OF CURRICULUM DISCIPLINES AND DISCIPLINED BEHAVIOR

If we are to go beyond providing recipes for "handling" child behavior problems, then we must consider the power of the curriculum content that children might learn in school. There are behavioral implications in curriculum planning and provisioning. We propose that when you wed content with concrete, meaningful activities you create disciplined behavior. By content, we mean knowledge that children acquire through activities. By concrete, meaningful activities, we mean those activities that stimulate children's feelings of accomplishment and responsibility. In this sense, curriculum is part of your behavior management system. In this sense, children learn what they live.

The applications of principles discussed in this book are embodied and summarized in the two sections that follow. In the first section, a teacher turns a chaotic classroom into a learning opportunity by focusing everybody's energies on content and building the children's sense of competence. The second section discusses computers in schools. While the computer represents one new technology that affects schools, there will be others. As you face new resources and approaches, it is helpful to apply some of the principles discussed in the book with the computer as one example.

A Sample Curriculum for Self-Direction

A sixth-grade class in which children had limited academic skills and were highly volatile, quick to jump into any possible physical conflict, lost their teacher to an extended, chronic illness during the academic year. The children were socially aware of one another and were very anxious to impress one another (and their adult onlookers) with their own competence.

The problem was that they were not competent in many socially accepted behaviors. They had trouble reading and completing traditional academic tasks. Instead, they had highly developed skills in verbally putting down one another, in recounting up-to-date sports results, in discussing the latest pop music, in displaying creative dance steps, and in commenting on each others' current clothes and hair arrangements.

The teacher who took over mid-year found that the students were using a current events newsletter and social studies textbooks written at a fourth-grade reading level, which was too lofty for at least half the group. As an alternative, she decided to take their interest in people, style, and mores and to apply these commitments to a broader study of other cultures.

One component of this study culminated in a multicultural fiesta that included displays of varied aspects of different cultures. In order to prepare the displays, children chose which culture they would study and which displays they would create. For the least able readers, she created some text material. For all the children, in collaboration with the school librarian, there was a variety of reading material available at different levels of difficulty, audio cassettes, film strips, and numerous relevant pictures. Parents were also involved through some food preparation and loans of phonograph records, clothing, and other artifacts.

The success of these events lay in the opportunity for children to (1) make choices among cultures, materials, and products, (2) use materials other than books and paper alone, (3) focus their interest in personal appearance through costumes that were researched, and (4) display their competence by explaining exhibits to younger children in the school and to parents who were invited to the fiesta. They also danced and sang.

The multicultural fiesta project also serves as an example of how the activity could engage them independently rather than by a teacher's continuous reminders. There was a considerable period of time during which external teacher controls gradually diminished as children were increasingly involved in the activities for their own sake. Clearly the teacher was involved in breaking down the activities into manageable tasks and providing suitable materials. She helped to make a match between the students and the tasks.

Instead of students looking toward external monitoring, they could see for themselves when a task was completed and take away a sense of competence. There was opportunity for a variety of acceptable responses and products for the same curriculum objective—to learn more about other cultures.

Originally, the teacher found all this energy in a situation where children felt powerless to perform competently. By providing opportunities for them to exercise their own power to choose and to act within the larger curriculum plan, she stimulated more responsible, self-directed behavior. Before, she was in a no-win situation. With the alternative plan, the children had an opportunity to behave in school in more acceptable ways and she had ample occasions to serve as a sincere appreciator of their efforts and accomplishments.

Wedding Computers and Human Curriculum

Just as a sense of power in learning is more likely to make children feel more receptive to taking on challenges and risks in future learning, a sense of powerlessness also has behavioral consequences. Consider, for example, the case of computers in education. If they are to become another medium for workbook tasks, children will be less likely to be involved beyond the novelty of the moving parts. Indeed, when you see children using computer software that is little more than an electronic workbook, their behavioral "problems" and "need to be reminded" to return to task arise.

By contrast, when children are able to influence choices and direct the sequence of events or a stylus, they seem quite willing to keep on task. Given this medium, it is particularly important to be critical consumers in order to assure a truly active learning opportunity for children. Among the more interactive possibilities are such phenomena as "Electronic Mail"—part of the "Quill" microcomputer-based writing system (Shostack, 1984) and Turtle LOGO (Papert, 1980).

On the surface, computers appear to be a more active form of learning than some more traditional ways. However, they are ultimately only active or interactive when they can serve to help children make new connections or reduce drudgery as in editorial work with a word processor. For children who have special educational needs, the computer can serve as an additional form with which to review material and practice skills in an individual, private fashion.

Otherwise, we recommend that computer literacy should be taught through applications to the content areas, as relevant rather than as one more isolated basic skill. Computer use is not any more of a panacea than any other skill or medium that is used in isolation. We hold that humane decisions, aesthetic considerations, and most sensory experiences are best left to human limitations rather than to the limitations of a machine.

Indeed, for children whose social skills are not terrific or well-developed, there might be a tendency to assign the child to use a computer. The child who spends increasing amounts of time at a computer has not had an opportunity to associate with other children and to struggle into social skills. While it looks like a good solution for minimizing interruptions and creating opportunities to distract children who are disruptive, it is a limited notion unless there are other extended opportunities to engage in social activities during the day.

Throughout this book we have encouraged teachers to be planners, to think ahead, to take the initiative, and to prevent problems from developing. It is possible to view the computer as a challenge, to plan ahead for computer-assisted instruction, to find ways in which it can enhance learning and create new adventures, and to seek opportunities to integrate it into a worthwhile curriculum rather than to wall it away out of fear or to worship it out of ignorance.

It is likely that computers in school are not going to be an option. They are more likely a given. Rather than be passive recipients of the given, we encourage you to accept a more active challenge. Use it to meet your needs and move toward your objectives rather than to feel controlled by the medium.

This is certainly an area in which students and teachers can learn together and share a sense of exploring new avenues. While this image is a far cry from the excitement generated by *Raiders of the Lost Ark* or the teacher-entertainer conception, there is opportunity for the potential excitement of teachers and children being active learners in a cooperative, responsible partnership.

WHICH EVENTS WILL YOU HOST?

In order to create an environment where children can be more self-regulating and all human beings can have an enjoyable, cooperative, learning experience, we recommend that you imagine planning for a buffet-style classroom rather than a sit-down dinner. The host or hostess of a sit-down dinner works very hard during the dinner after planning a single menu, never sure that it serves the tastes or balances nutritional needs of all the guests. In contrast, the buffet planner devotes more thought to providing options beforehand, but can be a more active participant during the actual event, can circulate among guests, and be more carefree.

Consider the successful buffet as one where there are never enough chairs. Movement is only mildly kinetic and there are opportunities for different people to meet one another. The hosting role—and the teacher is the host in a classroom—is to see that everyone has a satisfying experience, is socially employed, and has some nourishment in hand. The host brings people and materials together in this flexible structure.

The analogy between a party and a classroom is only partial. A teacher would also want to ensure that children experience longer-term, deeper relationships with other people, and a varied menu of materials. To host adequately, you need to prepare and anticipate needs. For example, if you know that somebody has special dietary needs, cannot handle certain food or drink, then you plan for it as a caring person. Certainly, in either case, you would not want to see anybody leave with indigestion.

As you move in a buffet setting, or in a decentralized classroom, it helps to involve the guests/students in planning for and choosing their food and in meeting other people. The best parties have lots of positive feelings, touches of humor, a generally light touch, and expectations of success. The host would try to avert showdowns between guests, and would not consider backing a guest into a figurative or literal corner in an argument. Should such an unfortunate incident occur, the host would attempt to mediate and help the participants save face.

Hosting the Event in Your School

Examples and cases in this book are site specific. That is, these are ways of working that need to be applied *relative* to your own school context. Collegial support and administrative encouragement or cooperation may or may not be ideal. These are realities with which to cope rather than excuses with which to deny the embodiment of your personal values about education and your knowledge of how children learn.

The cases we have shared with you represent a small but representative range of problems that teachers have encountered. In order to appreciate what you can do with ongoing situations, it makes sense for you to consider the approaches adaptively rather than literally. For example, within the guidelines that we have presented, what may work with one of the cases cited could very well depend upon a tone of voice at a particular moment. The success of a strategy might also depend upon the demands that are placed upon you by other children who are nearby and the particular makeup of your class.

Real Constraints

If you have several Jeffreys (flitters—see chapter 5) in your class, you may need to apply more external control than feels comfortable from September through November, gradually increasing student responsibility as they demonstrate increasing readiness to be more self-directed. It is difficult, when a new classroom is created, to be able to offer as many ready-made options right away as you would like. You may be short of materials and may even need to use newspapers as drawing paper.

You may find yourself in a situation where you have hardly any information about individual youngsters since families are increasingly mobile. You may make many false starts in the trial-and-error process before developing a workable plan. You may have occasions where you may feel like stopping the world, getting off, and starting over again.

These constraints would simply require more energy and time on your part in order to reach more limited goals. Even with these kinds of constraints, the guidelines represented in this book can work for you in both regular and special education settings. Alternative strategies help if they can be dredged up when you need them. They also are more easily retrievable after some practice. But, beyond planned techniques and strategies, each teacher adapts intuitively in each interaction.

When a teacher's thoughtful conceptual framework and personal perspective work together for the children's benefit, we can trust that the results will often be effective, at least benevolent. If you can break down tasks, identify what you want to see more of, it can help you become a more effective appreciator, a key role. A teacher's most effective framework is couched in terms that help children to achieve a sense of personal accomplishment, a sense of success, and the power to influence their own lives.

CONCLUSIONS AND REFLECTIONS

In the case of classroom organization and management, practice does not make perfect. Human interaction is a volatile, unpredictable, kaleidoscopic, unending revelation. The wonderful feelings of surprise when your plans work well, your children are productive, you all feel satisfied, or reasons for laughter and delight emerge unexpectedly compensate for risking the imperfectability of the next event.

While perfection is evasive, teaching practice that takes into account the human need for a feeling of competence and personal power is practice that improves children's willingness to risk academic challenges and to grow increasingly civilized. Above all, it is useful to keep in mind that humans develop along unpredictable curves rather than straight lines. Teaching in a decentralized, intensely human way can be an on-going adventure around the unpredictable curves. We wish you many adventures, a sense of competence, and foreseeable unpredictability.

References
About the Authors
Index

References

Aaron, B., & Bostow, D. Indirect facilitation of on-task behavior produced by contingent free-time for academic productivity. *Journal of Applied Behavior Analysis*, 1978, *11*, 197.

Anglin, L., Jr., Goldman, R., & Anglin, J. *Teaching: What it's all about.* New York: Harper and Row, 1982.

Apple Computer Co. *Legends.* Cupertino, Calif.: Apple, 1982.

Barnes, E., Berrigan, C., & Biklen, D. *What's the difference? Teaching positive attitudes toward people with disabilities.* Syracuse, N.Y.: Human Policy Press, 1978.

Bassett, J., Blanchard, E., & Koshland, E. On determining reinforcing stimuli: Armchair versus empirical procedures. *Behavior Therapy*, 1977, *8*, 205–212.

Becker, W., Madsen, C., Arnold, C., & Thomas, D. The contingent use of teacher attention and praise in reducing classroom behavior problems. *Journal of Special Education*, 1967, *1*, 287–307.

Bellack, A., Kliebard, H., Hyman, R., & Smith, F., Jr. *The language of the classroom.* New York: Teachers College Press, 1966.

Bendick, J. *The first book of automobiles* (rev. ed.). New York: Franklin Watts, 1971.

Bessell, H., & Palomares, V. *Magic Circle methods in human development.* Activity guides. La Mesa, Calif.: Human Development Training Institute, 1972.

Blume, J. *Blubber.* New York: Dell, 1976.

Brewster, B. [M. Elting]. *The first book of baseball* (J. Bendick, Illus.). New York: Franklin Watts, 1963.

Broden, M., Copeland, G., Beasley, A., & Hall, R. Altering student responses through changes in teacher verbal behavior. *Journal of Applied Behavior Analysis*, 1977, *10*, 479–487.

Bronfenbrenner, U. *Two worlds of childhood: U.S. and U.S.S.R.* New York: Russell Sage Foundation, 1970.

Brophy, J. Teacher praise: A functional analysis. *Review of Educational Research*, 1981, Spring, 5–32.

Brophy, J. Classroom organization and management. In D. C. Smith (Ed.), *Essential knowledge for beginning educators.* Washington, D.C.: AACTE, 1983, 23–37.

Brown, M. *The noisy book* (R. Thomson, Illus.). New York: Scroll Press, 1973.

Burchard, S. H. *Walt Frazier* (P. Frame, Illus.). New York: Harcourt Brace Jovanovich, 1975.

Canter, L. *Assertive discipline: A take-charge approach for today's educators.* Seal Beach, Calif.: Canter & Associates, 1976.

Cazden, C. *Child language and education.* New York: Holt, Rinehart and Winston, 1972.

Chapman, V. *Let's go to a service station* (P. Frame, Illus.). New York: G. P. Putnam's Sons, 1974.

Charles, C. *Elementary classroom management.* New York: Longman, 1983.

Chomsky, N. *Language and mind* (enlarged ed.). New York: Harcourt Brace Jovanovich, 1972.

Clements, J., & Tracy, D. Effects of touch and verbal reinforcement on the classroom behavior of emotionally disturbed boys. *Exceptional Children*, 1977, *43*, 453–454.

Cobb, J. A. Relationship of discreet classroom behaviors to fourth-grade academic achievement. *Journal of Educational Psychology*, 1972, *63*, 74–80.

Cooper, J. *Measuring behavior.* Columbus, Ohio: Charles E. Merrill, 1981.

Craighead, W., Kazdin, A., & Mahoney, M. *Behavior modification.* Boston: Houghton-Mifflin, 1981.

Curran, E. If the object is learning. *American Education*, 1982, *18*, 15–18.

Dreikurs, R., Grunwald, B., & Pepper, F. *Maintaining sanity in the classroom.* New York: Harper & Row, 1981.

Dreikurs, R., & Cassel, P. *Discipline without tears.* New York: Hawthorne Books, 1972.

Duke, D. (Ed.). *Helping teachers manage classrooms.* Alexandria, Va.: Association for Supervision and Curriculum Development, 1982.

Educational Teaching Aids. *Mathematics Catalog.* Chicago (159 West Kinzie St.): Educational Teaching Aids, 1984.

Elementary Science Study, *Teacher's guide for mystery powders.* New York: McGraw-Hill, 1974.

Elementary Science Study. *Teacher's guide for pendulums.* New York: McGraw-Hill, 1976.

Fitzhugh, L. *Harriet the spy.* New York: Harper and Row, 1964.

Flack, M. *Ask Mr. Bear.* New York: Macmillan, 1958.

Fleuegelman, A. *The new games book.* Garden City, N.Y.: Doubleday & Co., 1976.

Fromberg, D. *The reactions of kindergarten children to intellectual challenge.* Unpublished doctoral dissertation, Teachers College, Columbia University, 1965.

Gadow, K. *Children on medication: A primer for school personnel.* Reston, Va.: Council for Exceptional Children, 1979.

Gerger, D. *Word find puzzles #1.* New York: Grosset and Dunlap, 1973.

Ginnott, H. *Between parent and teenager.* New York: Macmillan, 1969.

Ginnott, H. *Teacher and child.* New York: Macmillan, 1972.

Glasser, W. *Schools without failure*. New York: Harper and Row, 1969.

Gordon, W. *Synectics*. New York: Harper and Row, 1961.

Gordon, W., & Poze, T. *Strange and familiar*. Cambridge, Mass.: Porpoise Books, 1972.

Gordon, W. & Poze, T. *The metaphorical way of learning and knowing*. Cambridge, Mass.: Porpoise Books, 1973.

Greene, C. *I know you, Al* (B. Barton, Illus.). New York: Viking, 1975.

Grossman Publishers. *Jackdaws*. New York: Grossman, 1966.

Henriod, L. *Marie Curie* (L. Henriod, Illus.). New York: G. P. Putnam's Sons, 1970.

Henry, J. *Pathways to madness*. New York: Vintage, 1973.

Henry, J. L. *Marie Curie, discoverer of radium* (J. Martinez, Illus.). New York: Macmillan, 1966.

Hurwitz, J. *Much ado about Aldo* (J. Wallner, Illus.). New York: Wm. Morrow, 1978.

Isaacs, S. *Intellectual growth in young children*. London: Routledge and Kegan Paul, 1930.

Jones, F. The gentle art of classroom discipline. *National Elementary Principal*, 1979, *58*, 26–32.

Joyce, B. *New strategies for social education*. Chicago: Science Research Associates, Inc., 1972.

Koester, L., & Farley, F. Hyperkinesis: Are there classroom alternatives to drug treatments? *Elementary School Guidance & Counseling*, 1981, *16*, 91–97.

Kounin, J. *Discipline and group management in classrooms*. New York: Holt, Rinehart & Winston, 1970.

Kroth, R. *Communicating with parents of exceptional children*. Denver: Love Publishing, 1975.

Kroth, R., & Simpson, R. *Parent conferences as a teaching strategy*. Denver: Love Publishing, 1977.

Lahaderne, H. Attitudinal and intellectual correlates of attention: A study of four sixth-grade classrooms. *Journal of Educational Psychology*, 1968, *59*, 320–324.

Lecky, P. *Self-consistency*. Garden City, N.Y.: Anchor Books, 1969.

Lucasfilm Productions, *Raiders of the Lost Ark*. Written by Lawrence Kaskan, story idea conceived by George Lucas and Phil Kaufman; Steven Spielberg, director. Lucasfilm productions, 1981.

Luria, A. *The mind of a mnemonist*. (Lynn Solotaroff, Trans.). New York: Basic Books, 1968.

Mackay, D., Thompson, B., & Schaub, P. *Breakthrough to literacy teacher's manual*. New York: Longman, 1978.

Macmurray, J. *The self as agent*. London: Faber and Faber, 1969.

Madsen, C., Becker, W., & Thomas, D. Rules, praise and ignoring: Elements of elementary classroom control. *Journal of Applied Behavior Analysis*, 1968, *1*, 139–150.

Martin, L. S. "What does research say about open education?" In V. R. Rogers &

B. Church (Eds.), *Open education: Critique and assessment.* Washington, D.C.: Association for Supervision and Curriculum Development, 1975, 83–98.

May, R. *Power and innocence.* New York: W. W. Norton, 1972.

McClelland, D., Atkinson, J., Clark, R., & Lowell, E. *The achievement motive.* New York: Appleton-Century-Crofts, 1953.

McKown, R. *Marie Curie* (R. McKown, Illus.). New York: G. P. Putnam's Sons, 1971.

Meichenbaum, D. *Cognitive-behavior modification.* New York: Plenum Press, 1977.

Meyer, J. S. *Engines* (J. Teppich, Illus.). Cleveland, Ohio: World Publishing, 1962.

Milton Bradley Co. Candyland (game)

Milton Bradley Co. Fractions (game)

Montessori, M. *The Montessori method.* (A. E. George, Trans.). New York: Schocken Books, 1965.

Moore, O. K., & Anderson, A. R. The responsive environments project. In R. D. Hess & R. M. Bear (Eds.), *Early education.* Chicago: Aldine Publishing, 1968, 171–189.

Morrison, H. *The practice of teaching in the secondary school.* Chicago: University of Chicago Press, 1926.

Myrdal, G. *American dilemma.* New York: Harper and Row, 1962.

O'Leary, K., & O'Leary, S. (Eds.). *Classroom management.* New York: Pergamon Press, 1977.

Olsen, J. T. *Joe Namath, the king of football* (M. Salmela, Illus.). Chicago: Children's Press, 1974.

Papert, S. *Mindstorms.* New York: Basic Books, 1980.

Peters, R. S. *Ethics and education.* Glenview, Illinois: Scott, Foresman, 1967.

Piaget, J. *The psychology of intelligence* (M. Piercy & D. E. Berlyne, Trans.). London: Rowledge and Kegan Paul, 1950.

Piaget, J. *Logic and psychology* (W. Mays & F. Whitehead, Trans.). New York: Basic Books, 1957.

Piaget, J. & collaborators. *The moral judgment of the child* (M. Gabain, Trans.). New York: Free Press, 1965.

Piaget, J., & Inhelder, B. *The psychology of the child* (H. Weaver, Trans.). New York: Basic Books, 1969.

Premack, D. Reinforcement theory. In D. Devine (Ed.), *Nebraska Symposium on Motivation.* Lincoln: University of Nebraska Press, 1965, 123–180.

Raschke, D. *The relationship of internal-external control and operant reinforcement procedures with learning and behavior disordered children.* Unpublished doctoral dissertation, University of Wisconsin, 1979.

Raschke, D. Designing reinforcement surveys—Let the student choose the reward. *Teaching Exceptional Children,* 1981, *14,* 92–96.

Rey, H. *Curious George.* New York: Houghton Mifflin, 1973.

Rimm, D., & Masters, J. *Behavior therapy.* New York: Academic Press, 1979.

Rosenthal, R., & Jacobson, L. *Pygmalion in the classroom.* New York: Holt, Rinehart & Winston, 1968.

Rothstein, E. *Teaching writing: A developmental, systematic approach.* Nyack, N.Y.: Evelyn Rothstein Associates/The Write Track, 1981.

Rothstein, E., & Gess, D. *Easy writer.* Nyack, N.Y.: Evelyn Rothstein Associates/Creative Communication Resources, 1982.

Rowe, M. *Teaching science as continuous inquiry.* New York: McGraw-Hill, 1978.

Scholastic School Services, Inc. *Scholastic readers' choice collections catalog.* New York: Scholastic School Services, 1984.

Serbin, L. Teachers, peers, and play preferences: An environmental approach to sex typing in the preschool. In B. Sprung (Ed.), *Perspectives on non-sexist early childhood education.* New York: Teachers College Press, 1978, ch. 6.

Shaftel, F., & Shaftel, G. *Role playing for social values.* Englewood Cliffs, N.J.: Prentice-Hall, 1967.

Shannon, J. A measure of the validity of attention scores. *Journal of Educational Research,* 1942, 35, 623–631.

Shostack, R. (Ed.). *Computers in composition instruction.* Eugene, Ore.: International Council for Computers in Education, 1984.

Slobodkin, E. *Caps for sale.* Reading, Mass.: Addison-Wesley, 1947.

Sullivan, G. *Pass to win* (P. Crowell, Illus.). Chicago: Garrard Publishing, 1968.

Sulzur-Azaroff, B., & Mayer, G. *Applying behavior-analysis procedures with children and youth.* New York: Holt, Rinehart & Winston, 1977.

Weber, W., Roff, L., Crawford, T., & Robinson, C. *Classroom management.* Princeton: Educational Testing Service, 1983.

Weehawken Board of Education. *Individualized language arts* (2d ed.). Weehawken, N.J.: Weehawken School District, 1974.

Weil, M., Joyce, B., & Kluwin, B. *Personal models of teaching.* Englewood Cliffs N.J.: Prentice-Hall, 1978.

Williams, J., & Abrashkin, R. *Danny Dunn and the homework machine* (E. J. Keats, Illus.). New York: Archway Books, 1979.

Winett, R., & Winkler, R. Current behavior modification in the classroom: Be still, be quiet, be docile. *Journal of Applied Behavior Analysis,* 1972, 5, 499–504.

Wolsch, R. A. *Poetic composition through the grades.* New York: Teachers College Press, 1970.

Zentall, S. Optimal stimulation as a theoretical basis of hyperactivity. *American Journal of Orthopsychiatry,* 1975, 45, 549–563.

Zim, H. S. *What's inside of engines?* (R. Perlman, Illus.). New York: William Morrow and Co., 1953.

Zimmerman, E., & Zimmerman, T. The alteration of behavior in a special classroom situation. *Journal of the Experimental Analysis of Behavior,* 1962, 1, 59–60.

About the Authors

DORIS PRONIN FROMBERG is Professor of Elementary and Early Childhood Education and Director of Early Childhood Teacher Education at Hofstra University in Hempstead, New York. She is also a field-based curriculum and administration consultant to school districts. After having been a teacher and administrator in public and private schools, she received the Ed.D. at Teachers College, Columbia University. Her special interests are early childhood curriculum as well as school climate and classroom organization in relation to children's successful learning experiences. She has published monographs, articles, and a book entitled, *Early Childhood Education: A Perceptual Models Curriculum* (Wiley, 1977). She and Dr. Driscoll served for five years as a field-based team of educational consultants through the U.S. Department of Education's Teacher Corps program.

MARYANNE DRISCOLL is a psychologist and educational consultant. She received her Ph.D. from Columbia University. She has taught in the Department of Special Education and Rehabilitation at Hofstra University and in the Department of School Psychology at Teachers College, Columbia University. She has been a staff psychologist at New York Medical College and at community clinics. She practices extensively with children who have learning, behavior, and/or physical difficulties and their parents. As an educational consultant, she has worked with administrators, regular and special education teachers, support service personnel, and paraprofessionals. Her special interests are classroom management, communication between regular and special educators, and social skills development. She is a frequent lecturer for teacher and parent groups.

Index